ON INTEGRATION:

"When the flying saucers were sighted over Ann Arbor, Mich., the first reaction from one of the residents was, 'Dammit, there goes the neighborhood.'

" 'But the Jolly Green Giant has been well received in America,' I said.

" 'Yes, but he's in show business!' "

"Art Buchwald can be seen as a pretty remarkable thing. He has been consistently funny, consistently cool, consistently effective. . . . One realizes, with admiration, what a unique place he holds in his profession, how uniformly high has been the level of his writing, and how re-readable he is."
—*New York World Journal Tribune*

"If you were to make a list of the great humorists of the last century, you would have to give a high place to Art Buchwald."
—*Boston Herald*

Art Buchwald

Son of the Great Society

illustrated by *LASZLO MATULAY*

A FAWCETT CREST BOOK

Fawcett Publications, Inc., Greenwich, Conn.
Member of American Book Publishers Council, Inc.

THIS BOOK CONTAINS THE COMPLETE TEXT OF THE ORIGINAL HARDCOVER EDITION.

A Fawcett Crest Book reprinted by arrangement with G. P. Putnam's Sons

Library of Congress Catalog Card Number: 66-20264

PRINTING HISTORY
G. P. Putnam's Sons edition published September 2, 1956
First printing, September 1966
Second printing, October 1966
Third printing, December 1966

First Fawcett Crest printing, September 1967

Published by Fawcett World Library
67 West 44th Street, New York, N. Y. 10036
Printed in the United States of America

CONTENTS

INTRODUCTION

Every once in a while, when I have nothing better to do, I wonder what the country would be like if Barry Goldwater had been elected President of the United States. Based on his campaign and his speeches, it is a frightening thing to imagine.

The mind boggles when you think of it. For one thing, we would probably be bombing North Vietnam now if Goldwater were in office.

As I see it, this is what would have happened.

The Viet Cong would have blown up an American barracks. Using this as an excuse, Goldwater would immediately call for a strike on military bases in North Vietnam and announce a "new tit-for-tat policy." Democrats would be horrified and they would make speeches that Goldwater was "trigger-happy" and was trying to get us into a war with Red China.

But Goldwater would ignore the criticism, and to show he meant business, he would continue the raids, using not only Air Force bombers, but jets from the U.S. fleet. As time went on, the country would be shaken at the recklessness of Goldwater's plan, but he would explain through his Secretary of State that, instead of a "tit-for-tat" policy, we now intended to bomb North Vietnam in order to let Hanoi know that they could not support the Viet Cong without expecting retaliation.

Senators would get up in Congress and call for some sort of negotiations. But Goldwater, with his lack of restraint, would retort that there is nothing to negotiate and we would only be selling out Southeast Asia if we sat down at a table with the North Vietnamese and Red China.

Russia and France would call for a Geneva conference, but Goldwater would reject it.

Instead, he would recklessly announce that he was sending in a battalion of Marines with Hawk missiles to protect our airfields. His critics would claim he was escalating the war, but Goldwater would deny it. Instead he would bomb supply routes in Laos and Cambodia.

To explain these desperate actions, Goldwater would have the Defense and State Departments produce a "White Paper" justifying the attacks and proving that Hanoi was responsible for the revolution in South Vietnam. He would insist we had to support the Saigon generals, no matter how shaky they were.

The paper would be followed by more air strikes, using South Vietnamese planes as well as American B-57s.

The people who voted for Johnson would scream at their Republican friends, "I told you if Goldwater became President he'd get us into a war." But the Republicans would claim that Goldwater had no choice, that he, in fact, inherited the Vietnam problem from the Democrats and, if he didn't take a strong stand now, America would be considered a paper tiger.

It all seems farfetched when you read it and I may have let my imagination run away with itself, because even Barry Goldwater, had he become President, wouldn't have gone so far.

But fortunately, with President Johnson at the helm, we don't even have to think about it.

I. THIS IS THE GREAT SOCIETY?

REGRETS ONLY

Just as I was giving up all hope of being invited to the Presidential Inauguration, I received a large 8 x 10-inch envelope in the mail which said on it, INAUGURATION COMMITTEE—DO NOT BEND.

With hands trembling, I cut open the envelope and took out a gold-engraved invitation which said, "The Inaugural Committee requests the honor of your presence to attend and participate in the inauguration of Lyndon Baines Johnson as President of the United States of America and Hubert Horatio Humphrey as Vice-President of the United States of America on Wednesday, the Twentieth of January, One Thousand Nine Hundred and Sixty-Five in the City of Washington."

I'll have to admit it. I started to bawl. The President hadn't forgotten me and all I had done to get him the nomination in Atlantic City.

When I composed myself, I called my wife and told her we had been invited to the inauguration.

It was her turn to sob. "With all he has to do," she said, "he remembered us."

We both chuckled and then she said, "Where are we sitting?"

"It doesn't say on the invitation, but I would guess in his box, maybe behind the Supreme Court Justices."

"What should I wear?" she said.

"Go out and buy yourself a new suit. After all, it isn't every day we get invited to the inauguration of the President of the United States."

"How will we get there?"

"The White House will probably send a car, but if they don't, we'll hire a limousine."

"My fur is so dowdy," she said.

"So get a new fur coat. We'll probably be on television most of the time and I want you to look nice."

"It seems like a dream," she said.

"Well, it isn't a dream," I replied. "I have the invitation right here in front of me." I picked it up, and as I did a slip of paper fell out of it. I started to read it to myself. It began: "IMPORTANT NOTICE—The Souvenir Invitation to the Inaugural is in grateful recognition of the interest you have manifested in the election of the President and Vice-President of the United States. It conveys our sincere wish that you may be in Washington for the occasion, but the invitation in itself does NOT constitute an admission to any of the inaugural events."

The notice then went on to point out that the events were by separate invitation only and not to send a check unless you were invited by somebody else.

"Hello, hello," my wife said. "Are you still there?"

"You know what I said about a new suit?"

"Yes."

"Forget it."

"But what will I wear to the inauguration?"

"We're not going to the inauguration."

"But we were invited."

"That's how much you know," I said angrily. "And don't get that fur coat, either."

Later on I walked into the Washington bureau of the New York *Herald Tribune* and everyone, including the office boy, was holding one of the invitations in his hand.

"What do you think it all means?"

"It beats me," a reporter said. "But if you ask me, I think someone over at the White House got a new printing press for Christmas."

THIS IS THE GREAT SOCIETY?

It was very heartening to discover that President Johnson had to borrow money to pay his income taxes. I wish the President no ill and my heart goes out to anyone who has to borrow money to pay taxes, particularly myself, but in this case the President started all the trouble, and he has only himself to blame.

As I see it, everyone's troubles began because of the tax cut the President instituted. Before he started talking cuts, most Americans were so numb paying taxes that they didn't even think about it. Every time their wives said they wanted to buy something, the husbands would bark, "You can't. We're in terrible trouble on taxes."

All of us had made up our minds there was no out, and we were getting used to our standard of living, no matter what it was.

Then, with the election coming along, the President in an impassioned plea asked Congress to give the American people tax "relief." He said that if taxes were reduced the economy would be given a great impetus. He promised that people would spend more money, the gross national product would soar, jobs would be created, and America would be a better country for us all.

Congress responded, as it usually does when the President speaks, and after only a moderate job of arm-twisting, the President's tax-cut bill was passed.

The President was overjoyed and he signed the bill while cameras turned and photo bulbs flashed.

The ink was hardly dry on the paper when American wives went berserk. They started looking for new homes, new furniture; they ordered new draperies, new automobiles; they took their kids out of public schools and put them in private schools.

Many wives decided to go to Europe, other wives gave large black-tie dinner parties. The economy zoomed as the President predicted. The gross national product increased, employment went up, and everyone at the White House said, "Mr. President, you've done it again."

But no one ever bothered to check how much the tax cut would mean to each individual. All we kept reading about was an $11,500,000 tax cut, and so every wife in America thought each husband was entitled to the $11,500,000.

No one bothered to prorate it. When they finally did, they discovered their tax cut came to about $18.90.

By this time it was too late. Mortgages had been signed, car financing had been arranged, department stores refused to take back the furniture. Everyone's living standard had risen and no one wanted to go back to the pre-tax-cut days.

So here we are in the midst of the biggest boom in American history and everyone from the President of the United States down is eyeball-to-eyeball with his bank, all because Lyndon Johnson wanted the American people to have a tax cut.

If he had just left us alone, we could have all made our tax payments this year.

What worries me more than anything else is that Sheldon Cohen, the Commissioner of Internal Revenue, has promised tax relief to those who can't make their payments on time. When my wife read about this, she said, "Well, as long as they don't want the money right away, I think I'll buy a new rug."

Please, Mr. President, don't talk about any more tax relief. None of us can afford it.

FRIENDLY PERSUASION

The settlement of the steel strike was another feather in the cap of President "I Won't Take No for an Answer" Johnson. The negotiations were hard and they were tense and I can now reveal for the first time how the President got the parties to agree.

On Monday he asked both management and the union officials to come to Washington. The men were met at the airport in black limousines and immediately driven to the White House, where they were ushered into a large bare office with a table and hard chairs. The President greeted them, told them of his desire for a just settlement, and offered the use of his executive offices to continue the negotiations. Both sides thanked the President for his kind offer but said they preferred to continue the talks in Pittsburgh.

"That's fine with me," the President said, and then he left the room. But when the union and management people tried to leave the room, the first person to the door shouted in panic, "It's locked!"

Several of the steel and union executives tried the door without success.

Then someone said, "Let's go out the window." Just below the window were four marines with fixed bayonets. They started to raise their rifles.

The negotiators sat down at the table.

On Tuesday one of the President's aides came into his office and said, "Sir, they're asking for food."

"Tell them they can have all the food they want, even from the White House kitchen, as soon as they sign a contract."

"Yes, sir."

"By the way, did you turn off the air conditioning?"

"Yes, sir. And we put heat in the radiators, as you suggested."

"That's just fine."

The next morning Mr. Johnson's secretary came in. "There are some officials from the International Red Cross outside, sir."

"Send them in."

The first official spoke. "Mr. President, we understand you're violating the Geneva Convention in regard to the treatment of union and management officials who have been captured by you."

"The reports have been exaggerated," the President said. "Ah've treated them justly and fairly."

"We understand they haven't eaten in three days and there is even a shortage of water. We also understand they have not been allowed to contact their relatives and have been unable to talk to a representative of the Red Cross."

"Ah've never used force on anyone," Mr. Johnson said. "When they put their country ahead of their own needs, as true Americans, I will release them and send them back to their loved ones. Good day, gentlemen."

On Thursday an aide reported again. "Three have passed out from the union side and two from management. One executive is seeing mirages, and another union official is yelling at the marines to shoot him. I believe a settlement is near."

"Notify the television networks to stand by. We may have a break in the next 48 hours. And, Jack, take the chairs out of the room and make them stand for a while."

On Friday, at exactly six o'clock, an aide came dashing in.

"They've agreed to settle, sir."

"Good. What have they agreed on?"

"They said you announce it and they'll sign it. All they ask is food, water, and a bed."

"Bring 'em out first to appear in front of television, Jack, and be sure and clean them up. I don't want the people to think I used any pressure on them while they were negotiating."

A CASE FOR FLU

Everyone was delighted with the fast recovery of President Lyndon B. Johnson from his gall bladder operation. I myself wish the President had taken it a little easier after the operation and this is why.

I came down with the flu over a weekend and ordinarily in these situations my wife is very sympathetic. But not this time. I told her I planned to stay in bed for the day and maybe watch a couple of football games and the World Series until my temperature went down.

She showed me a newspaper and said, "The President had a gall bladder operation and look what he did. He appointed four ambassadors, two judges, saw Vice-President Humphrey, talked to the press, and signed three bills, and you want to stay in bed just because you have a little flu."

"But he's stronger than I am," I protested. "Besides, they say flu can be serious."

She turned to another part of the paper. "Here is a picture of Mr. Johnson's gall bladder with the stone still in it. And yet do you know what he's going to do tomorrow if the doctors let him?"

"What?"

"Dictate his budget for 1966, inspect the Bethesda Naval Hospital, talk to Dean Rusk and Robert McNamara, telephone seven astronauts, and address a joint session of Congress in the operating theater of the hospital. And you're complaining about a little fever."

"It isn't just the fever. I feel kind of groggy too."

"How can you feel groggy after what the President went through? I just heard on the radio that if all goes well, the day after, the President plans to meet with the National Security Council, hold a press conference, attend a barbecue at the hospital for doctors and their wives, talk to the United Nations, and help Mrs. Johnson plant twelve trees along the Belt Parkway. I don't see why you should feel sorry for yourself."

"I'm not feeling sorry for myself," I said. "It's just that the flu takes a lot out of you."

"Are you trying to say that a gall bladder operation doesn't take a lot out of a person? Listen to the President's schedule for Thursday. He's having breakfast with the Senate and House leaders, meeting with labor leaders on 14B, lunching with the League of Women Voters, making a film for a fund-raising dinner in California, and attending an enlisted men's dance at the Bethesda USO Club."

"Okay, I'll go out and cut the lawn," I said.

"If you want to stay in bed, I'm perfectly agreeable," my wife said, "but it seems to me you're not showing much moral fiber. Here's the President's schedule for Friday."

"I don't want to hear it," I said, slowly putting on my shoes.

"The President is going to sign several more bills, attend the opening of a new ward, settle the India-Pakistan dispute, and if he has time perform an appendectomy on a lieutenant commander."

I started shaking as I tried to put on my shirt.

"Where should I put the leaves after I rake them up?" I asked.

"There is no reason to be surly. If you really don't feel well, stay in bed."

I went back to bed.

"Is there anything I can get you?" she asked.

"Yeah. Get me Vice-President Humphrey. I'll talk to him first. Then you can let the press in. I'll talk to the Joint Chiefs of Staff this afternoon, and tonight if I feel up to it we'll take down all the billboards along Wisconsin Avenue. There is no sense letting a little flu bug get me down."

THE SLEEP GAP

No one in Washington is talking about it, but there is a sleep gap in the Johnson Administration and it's getting more serious all the time. The President, who according to reports doesn't need much sleep because of extra glands, makes no secret of his admiration for those who are able to operate on as little sleep as he does. Time and time again he has praised those who are in their offices at seven in the morning and don't leave until very late at night.

I can well imagine what is happening at a Cabinet meeting these days.

All the Cabinet officers are in their chairs dozing—waiting for the President to arrive.

He enters the room, and everyone tries to wake up.

"Well, gentlemen," the President says, "it's good to see you all looking so haggard and bleary-eyed. We're getting a lot done."

The Attorney General stifles a yawn.

"Were you trying to say something, Mr. Katzenbach?"

"No, sir, Mr. President. I was just yawning."

"Good boy. You're doing a fine job. Well, let's get down to business. I'd like to discuss the opposition we're getting in the Senate. Mr. McNamara. Will somebody wake up Mr. Mc-Namara?"

Mr. McNamara says, "Uh-wha-uh, oh, yes, sir, Mr. President."

"Mr. McNamara," the President says, "when I called you at three this morning, your wife said you had already gone to bed."

"Yes, sir, I was at the Pentagon until two, so I decided to make an early night of it."

"Well, it isn't important. I'm sorry your wife woke you up."

"That's all right, sir."

"It was the four o'clock call that was important. You can imagine my surprise when I found out that you had gone back to sleep."

"I wasn't really sleeping, sir. I just had my eyes closed waiting for your next call."

"Anyway, that's neither here nor there. Mr. Rusk."

Mr. Rusk is going, "Zzzz, zzzzzz, zzzzzz."

One of Mr. Rusk's aides shakes him.

"I called the State Department at 6:30 this morning, Mr. Rusk, and you hadn't arrived yet. Something wrong at home?"

"No, sir. I just went to the dentist and hadn't gotten in yet. Was there anything special, Mr. President?"

"Well, when you left the White House at 2:30 this morning, I still had a couple of questions to ask you about Vietnam."

"You should have called me at home."

"At that hour? Come to think of it, I tried to, but someone took the phone off the hook."

"It must have been one of the servants, sir."

"It doesn't make any difference. I called the Vice-President instead. He sounded very chipper. I was surprised. Apparently I'm still not giving Hubert enough to do."

The President then turns to his Postmaster General. "Mr. O'Brien, you look wide awake."

"I'm sorry to give that impression, sir. I'm dead tired."

"How much sleep did you get last night?"

"Five hours, sir, but I slept fitfully."

"All right, gentlemen, I guess that winds up the Cabinet meeting. Let's all meet back here at one in the morning, unless any of you have something better to do."

The Cabinet members all put their Benzedrine capsules away as one of them says, "What else could we possibly have to do?"

DON'T PHONE US

After it was announced that Marvin Watson had been put in charge of security at the Executive Mansion and was logging everyone's telephone calls, reporters began to refer to the White House as "Stalag 1600."

The excuse given for checking calls was that a special study was being made to see how many telephone lines the White House really needs.

Well, it turns out that the survey is over and now, according to Mr. Bill Moyers, the White House expects to save $6,000 a month in telephone charges.

Many special assistants had their lines cut down and a few who received no calls at all during the survey had their telephones taken away from them altogether.

As a matter of fact, the day after the economies were put into effect, the President called in Marvin Watson and said:

"Marv, I can't seem to get Jack on the phone."

"He doesn't have a phone anymore, sir. We found out during the survey he got exactly three calls: two were from his wife asking him when he was going to be home and one was from his wife saying she was leaving home."

"Well, how do I get in touch with him?" the President asked.

"We have these pigeons, sir. You just write a message and attach it to a leg. Jack will get it within the hour."

"That's a good idea, Marv. I'll tell Bill to announce it at the briefing. His line's busy."

"Bill has only one line now, Mr. President. It appears every newspaperman in the world was calling him up and we figured it might discourage them if they couldn't get through."

"What happens if I need Bill in a hurry?" the President said.

"We're installing a drum in your office. You beat on it and, as each office along the way hears the signal, they'll pass it on and Mr. Moyers will eventually hear it and come running. He can also beat out a message to you when he has something on his mind."

"That makes sense. What is that I hear about the telephones being taken out of the War Room?"

"They never got any calls down there, sir, and I figured we could save $600."

"What happens in an emergency?"

"We have a bonfire ready to go at any time in the rose garden. When you wave this flag, an Indian with a blanket will be alerted to send out smoke signals. Another Indian stationed in the War Room will be able to reply. It's absolutely foolproof."

"Good boy, Marv. I notice you took out all the phones in the East wing of the White House. How do we keep in touch with them?"

"We have a Pony Express rider stationed right outside the West Wing door. He will deliver a pouch back and forth three times a day."

"That makes sense," the President said. "What if Lady Bird wants to speak to me?"

"The Army engineers have built this system. You see, these are two ordinary soup cans. There is a waxed string attached to each end. When you talk in one end, Mrs. Johnson can hear you and she can reply the same way."

"I'll be darned," the President said.

Just then Luci walked in. "What happened to my phone?" she demanded.

The President looked at Mr. Watson. "Marv, you didn't take her phone away, too?"

"You said to take out everything but the Hot Line."

"Give Luci her phone back—and, Marv, take out the Hot Line instead."

LOBBYING WITH THE FIRST LADY

There has been a lot of talk about President Johnson's arm-twisting when it comes to Congress, but very little has been said about Mrs. Johnson's persuasive powers with that same body.

Mrs. Johnson is very interested in legislation that has to do with beautifying America and she came all the way to Jackson Hole to dramatize the cause.

The bill she is seeking is now being considered by Congress and a spokesman for Mrs. Johnson said that the First Lady called several Congressmen to "thank" them for their help.

I haven't been privy to any of these conversations, but I would guess they may have gone something like this.

"Hello, Congressman Jones, this is Lady Bird Johnson calling."

"Oh, how do you do, Mrs. Johnson."

"Ah just called to thank you for everything you've done to help get H. R. 8701 through Congress."

"Yes, yes, well, uh . . ." (Aside to his secretary: "Find out what the heck H. R. 8701 is all about.") "I'm certainly glad to oblige, Mrs. Johnson."

"Ah told Lyndon, just this morning at breakfast, that Congressman Jones could be counted on our side, not only to get it out of committee, but to a vote."

"What did the President say, Mrs. Johnson?"

"He said, 'Congressman Jones has never let us down before, so there is no reason on God's good green earth why he'd let us down now.' "

(Congressman to secretary, "Did you ever find out what the bill is?") "All of us up here on the Hill are for you, Mrs. Johnson. I was just telling Betty this morning at breakfast how interested we were in your legislation."

"Ah spoke to Betty at lunch. She told me she was sure that you would be able to work something out that would be satisfactory to all the women of America."

"Betty said that?"

"Yes, she said that she was surprised you hadn't done anything about the bill before now and she planned to discuss it with you tonight."

"Well, you know, Mrs. Johnson, it's fortunate you called at this moment because I was just going over the bill with my staff." (Aside to secretary, "Look in the other files. The bill's got to be somewhere.")

"Lyndon said you would probably get to it today or tomorrow and he suggested Ah wait until you get it out of committee before Ah thanked you, but Ah told him Ah knew you were going to do the right thing and Ah wanted to thank you in advance."

"That's awfully nice of you, Mrs. Johnson."

"Lyndon said you've got that dam you want so badly on your mind that you might have forgotten about mah little old bill, but Ah said Ah was sure Congressman Jones would put mah bill before his dam."

"The President's right, Mrs. Johnson. Without your bill, my dam would have no meaning at all."

"Well, thanks so much, Congressman Jones. You and Betty must come over sometime and have a meal with us."

"Yes, ma'am. Anytime."

He hangs up. "Miss Smith, report H. R. 8701 out on the floor today."

"But don't you even want to read it?"

"Don't ask any questions, and if my wife calls, tell her I've already got the message."

WE INTERRUPT THIS PROGRAM

President Johnson has been going on television so much that it isn't too farfetched to predict that in the near future the networks might announce, while the President was speaking, "We interrupt this regular program to bring you an important announcement."

It is no secret that the networks are very upset about the President asking for time on short notice to address the American people. For one thing it's quite costly and for another you don't know what to believe in *TV Guide* anymore.

Several compromises are trying to be worked out between

the White House and the three major networks. One of them has been to offer the President his own show. The White House is interested, provided the President can get prime time, but the networks want to put him on after Johnny Carson.

Also the format of the show has to be worked out. One network has offered to call the program "I've Got a Secret." It would be a panel show and the panel would have to guess where the President was going to send the Marines next.

Another network wants the President to appear in a situation comedy titled "I Love Luci" and dramatize the problems of a typical American family whose father happens to be President of the United States.

The third network wants to call the show "Have Guns—Will Travel," which would be a Western with most of the action taking place at the LBJ Ranch and the Pentagon.

So far the President hasn't agreed to any of the formats. He also is against a regular time slot because if he went along with it, he could only appear on TV once a week, and this could become too confining.

There is also a question of sponsorship. If the President went on television regularly the networks insist they would have to sell the time to a sponsor. A dog food company has expressed interest in the show provided the President would appear with his beagle.

Several aspirin companies have put in a bid for the time and so have insurance companies. The only ones who definitely said they weren't interested were the electric light bulb companies, who felt the image just wouldn't be right for them.

Another problem is the question of ratings. The White House is aware that the networks will drop a show without hesitation if the ratings are low. So they're demanding some guarantee from the networks that they won't cancel out after the first 13 weeks, particularly since President Johnson's term has a few years to go.

The networks claim they have no choice when it comes to ratings and they would be setting a bad precedent if they allowed a show with low ratings to remain on the air. As the owner of a television station, the networks feel, the President should understand this.

Finally, there is the question of the Early Bird satellite. If the European networks clear time for President Johnson on their stations then the American networks will have to clear time for the European leaders.

Between Chancellor Erhard, Prime Minister Harold Wilson and General de Gaulle, the networks are frightened that they may not have any audience left. They've tried to persuade President Johnson to stay off the Early Bird satellite, but so far without success.

The President has already told the network bosses:

"Ah didn't put it up there just to look at, and any time Ah want to Ah can have the Air Force shoot it down."

SINCERELY YOURS

It is not generally known, but when somebody leaves the White House, every President writes two letters. One is for the public record and the other is for the personal use of the person being fired.

In the first letter the President tries to give the impression he is sad to see the person go. In the second letter the President tries to spell out the reasons why the person's leaving is no great loss.

I have never seen any of the latter letters, but I can imagine they go something like this:

DEAR JOHN,

Marv Watson advises me we are short on space in the east wing of the White House. As you recall, when I first became President, I said I needed you very badly. Valenti informs me we need the space more.

For one thing we plan on appointing a woman to your position, and, since the east wing of the White House will be entirely turned over to the female side of the staff, we will be unable to provide men's washroom facilities. I feel it would be too time-consuming for you to run over to the west wing every time you wanted to wash your hands.

I know you're wondering why I'm writing this letter. Let me say you have heard me state many times I don't want to be a great President; I just want to be a good President—therefore, I really don't need you.

This is not to say you haven't done a good job. The speeches you have written were exactly what I wanted—

homespun, heartwarming, and chock-full of statistics.

I liked the way you handled my references to the ranch and my descriptions of the Pedernales River. I even enjoyed that part about my being the great wound healer in that speech you wrote for the Hod Carriers Union.

But, John, there is one thing I ask in return for allowing someone to work for me 18 hours a day seven days a week—and that's loyalty. No one was more surprised than I was when you asked, out of the clear blue sky, if you could stay home with your family on Christmas Day. You put me in a terrible spot, John. You made me feel as if I was keeping you away from your loved ones on a day that was dear to all of us. You remember what I said then? I said, "John, you know you can spend Christmas with your family. By all means, take it off if it will make you happy. I'll write the Great Society speech myself."

I know you didn't take Christmas off, John, and you did work on the speech, but the thing that really hurt was that you wanted to take the day off.

And then there was the other matter. On two occasions, one at two in the morning and the other time at three, I found you in your office sleeping at your desk. I didn't mind your sleeping at your desk, but why, John, did you leave the lights on? I asked you why you left the lights on and you said you hadn't been to bed for 36 hours, which I thought even then was a pretty poor excuse for wasting the taxpayers' money.

I want to add I have always been impressed by your modesty, your dedication, and your earnestness. It was your dancing I never liked.

So this letter is to thank you for your services and to tell you to take all the time you want to clean out your desk. Watson says we don't need the office until Friday.

Oh, by the way, in case you're going to write your memoirs about working for me, I hope you'll remember it was your choice to work Christmas Day, and not mine.

Sincerely yours,

BAD NEWS FOR HUBERT

People in Washington believe one of the reasons President Johnson hasn't been reporting to the American people is that he likes to announce only good news. If unemployment goes down, a railroad strike is settled, or Congress passes an Administration bill, the President is the first to reveal it. But when things are going badly, the President feels that the American people shouldn't know about it.

What complicates matters for everyone is that, because of his delivery, even when the President is announcing good news, it sounds like bad news.

Therefore, what the President needs is someone to announce the bad news for him. We think the perfect candidate for this job would be Vice-President Hubert Humphrey. The reason for this is that, because of Mr. Humphrey's cheery personality, even when he announces bad news, it sounds like good news.

As I see it, the President would call Mr. Humphrey into his office and say, "Hubert, here are the things I want you to announce to the press today—the South Vietnamese government has been overthrown, gold reserves are down, there may be a steel strike, and 300 more Negroes were arrested in Selma, Alabama."

"Yes, sir, Mr. President, it will be a breeze," the Vice-President replies. "Is that all the bad news you've got?"

"It's been a dull day for bad news. I'll probably have more for you tomorrow."

"Mr. President, I don't like to complain, but last week Bob McNamara announced that in case of a nuclear war 120 million Americans would be killed. I think I should have announced that, since bad news is my province."

"Well, McNamara's been announcing bad news for so long, it's hard to get him to stop. I'll speak to him about it and see if he could throw some bad news your way."

"Also, Mr. President, Dean Rusk announced that the Chinese would soon explode another atomic bomb. This was one of the biggest bad news stories of the week. I called Rusk about it and he said you had told him to go ahead and announce it."

"You were out of town, Hubert, and I didn't think it could wait. Since I didn't want to announce it, I felt as a matter of protocol Rusk should be allowed to do it."

"But since you announced that I would be in charge of bad news, and you allowed Rusk to announce the China bomb explosion, the press is claiming that you have no confidence in me."

"That's ridiculous, Hubert, and to prove it I'm going to let you go on television and explain what a mess we're in in the Congo."

"I'd be most grateful for that, sir."

"Good. On the same television show I would also like you to describe the impasse in the United Nations, the number of American embassies that have been stoned since we bombed North Vietnam, and President de Gaulle's plans to undermine NATO."

"That's wonderful, Mr. President."

"I'll go on television right after you."

"What are you going to announce, Mr. President?"

"My new plan to beautify Washington, D.C., the name of the next Ambassador to Nepal, and a new tax cut for the women's toiletries industry."

PROCLAIMING MOTHER'S DAY

Last May, President Johnson issued a Mother's Day proclamation, urging all people to express their love and gratitude for their mothers. The story behind this decision can now be told.

For weeks, rumors had been rampant in Washington that the President would declare May 9 Mother's Day. But no high official was willing to confirm it. All queries were referred to the White House.

At his press briefing Bill Moyers said he knew nothing about the President's making a Mother's Day proclamation and, to his knowledge, the President had no plans to declare it an official holiday. When reporters persisted in questioning Mr. Moyers on the subject, he was quoted as stating, "That's all I have to say on the matter at this time."

In the meantime, the President was meeting with National Security Adviser McGeorge Bundy and Secretary of Defense

McNamara to discuss the various possibilities. While Secretary of State Rusk was not at the meeting, he was kept informed as to what was going on.

McNamara and Bundy both argued that something had to be done about Mother's Day before May 9 and that the President should be the one to explain it to the American people.

The first thing the President did was to call Congressional leaders to the White House and inform them of his decision. Both Senators Mike Mansfield and Everett Dirksen pledged their support to the President as did Representatives Carl Albert and Gerald Ford.

Senator Dirksen was quoted as telling the President, "It's the only thing you can do under the circumstances."

Senator Mansfield said, "Except for Senator Wayne Morse, I believe the Democratic majority will back you."

After the Congressional leaders left the White House, President Johnson telephoned former President Eisenhower and told him what he was going to do about Mother's Day.

President Eisenhower said, "If I were in your position, Mr. President, I would do exactly the same thing. I will issue a statement giving my wholehearted approval."

The President then telephoned former President Truman, who said, "It's about blankety-blank time! If anybody says anything about your decision, I'll tell them where to go."

The next call the President made was to former Senator Barry Goldwater. Mr. Goldwater pointed out that during his campaign he had always advocated a strong Mother's Day policy, and he was glad to see the President was finally following it. Mr. Goldwater said the President could count on him.

During the next week the President had Lou Harris, Sam Lubell, and George Gallup take polls to see what the consensus of the American people was in regards to a Mother's Day proclamation. Seventy-five percent of the people said they believed in Mother's Day, 5 percent were against it, and 20 percent said that they had no opinion.

Encouraged by the polls, the President decided to act.

He alerted two airborne divisions, four Marine brigades, and the Atlantic Fleet in case there would be any trouble. He then arranged for Secretary McNamara, Undersecretary of State George Ball and McGeorge Bundy to appear on television before him to explain his Mother's Day policy.

Then he made the announcement himself at a hurriedly

called press conference. At this writing, the reaction in the United States was very good, though there was still some question as to whether our allies would support the Mother's Day proclamation. So far both France and the Soviet Union had said they wouldn't.

INFLATION HITS THE JOHNSONS

Last Thursday, President Johnson asked the American people to stop spending so much money on themselves. He said that if we continued spending at the rate we were, we would be inviting inflation. To dramatize his leadership in this fight he told a group of mayors and urban leaders: "I asked Mrs. Johnson this morning, (*sic*) even as she has changed cooks, is she exercising all the care in her buying that she did in times that weren't so prosperous.

"I remember a lot of times when I had a different kind of meat. Sometimes it was meat of a kind I didn't like. It was a cheaper cut. . . . I just wonder if the women of this country couldn't get out their lead pencils and put on their glasses and look at some of those price lists and see where these shortages are occurring and see where these prices are advancing and say 'good-bye to those products going up.' Just say 'I don't have to have that. I will just substitute.'"

The scene, of course, is the White House. The President is dining with Lady Bird alone.

"Lady Bird, this tastes like a pretty good piece of meat to me. You getting extravagant again?"

"Now, Lyndon. We've been eating the leftovers from Madame Gandhi's dinner for two weeks and I thought it was about time we had a change."

"I guess you're right. By the way, did you know A & P is having a sale on pork rib ends?"

"Lyndon, you hate pork rib ends."

"I know I do. But my country comes first. Please pass the lower-priced spread."

"Lyndon, the President of Costa Rica is coming next week and the new chef wanted to know if you're serious about serving meat loaf for the main course."

"I've been giving it a lot of thought, Lady Bird. I just read where Safeway Stores got in a shipment of neckbones. Ask the chef what he can do with those."

"Oh, for heaven's sake, Lyndon, the chef almost quit the other night when you made him prepare Vienna sausages for the House and Senate Democratic Leaders' dinner. Please don't ask him to cook neckbones."

"All right, we'll stick with the meat loaf and cut out the salad. By the way, this bread tastes awfully fresh."

"It was baked today, Lyndon. They ran out of day-old bread at the bakery."

"I'll bet they just told you that so they could sell you fresh bread. Well, take out your lead pencil and put on your glasses and let's say good-bye to a few products that are going up in price."

"Lyndon, we've eliminated practically everything."

"You can always find more. I think we better eliminate stewed tomatoes, okra, and broccoli for a while."

"Luci loves okra."

"Well, the kids today have to make a few sacrifices. When I was her age I only had okra once a month, if we were lucky."

"All right, Lyndon. What should we have instead?"

"Orville Freeman tells me I can get a good buy on turnip greens."

"Lyndon, there's something I wanted to bring up at this time. It's Luci's wedding cake. Do you still insist it be made with powdered eggs?"

"Well, if she really feels strongly about it, I guess we can use fresh eggs. After all, your daughter only gets married once."

PARTY TALK IN WASHINGTON

In a speech recently, President Johnson said that every time you go to a party these days in Washington all people talk about is inflation.

I wasn't aware this was the main topic in the capital, but after reading the President's speech, I boned up on inflation so I wouldn't look like a fool the next time I went to a party.

Last week, as luck would have it, I was invited to a large dinner gathering of very distinguished people.

During the cocktail hour I wandered up to a group of men talking in hushed tones.

"I see where the economy is dangerously perking to fever heat," I said.

They ignored me completely. One man said, "Well, if you think the skirts are short in your department you ought to come over to my office. It's enough to make a man climb right up the wall."

"I won't allow my secretary to sit down anymore when she's taking dictation," another man said.

"Can't say I blame you."

I tried to get back into the conversation. "The President said we can't allow the last five years of unprecedented prosperity to be endangered and swallowed up by inflation."

I received several hostile looks. One of the men said, "It isn't just the daytime that is driving me crazy. You go out in the evening and all you see is large holes in the dresses covered with black net. I mean, what is a man supposed to do?"

"I believe the only thing to do is become a sex maniac. After all, you have to keep up with the times."

I wandered away from the group and went up to several women who were sipping cocktails. I said, "As I see it, the main problem of inflation is to put your foot on the brakes, without going into a skid of recession."

Several of the women tittered. One of them said, "Where was I before I was interrupted? Oh yes, so he had a girl friend in the Pentagon and his wife found out about it. She immediately demanded a divorce, but he asked for another chance."

"Speaking of another chance," I said, "some economists say if we could take five billion dollars out of the economy without raising taxes we could stabilize prices."

There was an embarrassed silence. Then one of the women said, "That wasn't the first time he got caught, you know. He went to Florida with a translator from the World Bank, and his wife found out about that."

"It could have been worse," I said. "One of the main problems we have is tourists going abroad, which is playing havoc with the gold flow. If more people would go to Florida the dollar would be strengthened."

I received nothing but cold stares so I went over to a third group. "If they send Ginzburg to jail," one of the men was saying, "what is the Supreme Court going to do about the publishers of *Candy?*"

"Has anyone read *The Story of O?* That beats them all."

"I didn't read it," I said, "but I did read in *Fortune* that if we show self-restraint in spending and defer capital investments, we would not need any price or wage controls."

The group broke up immediately.

I stood around looking for someone to talk to when my wife came up to me. "If you don't behave yourself I'm going home."

"What did I do?"

"The hostess says you've been saying the most outrageous things and embarrassing everybody."

"I was just trying to discuss inflation like the President said we were supposed to do."

"Why don't you save that kind of talk for your locker room friends?"

"All right," I said, and I went over to the bar.

"Anybody heard anything new on Bobby Baker lately?"

Several people smiled. "Come on in and have a drink."

II. THE AGONIZING
COLUMNIST

FEAR IN THE WHITE HOUSE

The appointment of John Chancellor, the NBC White House correspondent, as the new director of the Voice of America, dramatically announced by President Johnson at a news conference, has struck fear in the hearts of all newspapermen covering the White House beat.

It is no secret that the President has done everything in his power to win the press over to his side, but no one dreamed he would go as far as to start appointing them to public office.

In the past a telephone call from the President in the middle of the night to a newspaperman either meant Mr. Johnson was pleased or displeased with a story, but now it could mean the President wants to appoint him to a job in the Administration.

This has caused all sorts of dilemmas for the White House correspondents.

I can just imagine the scene in a few weeks from now.

It's twelve o'clock at night and the phone rings in the bedroom of a White House correspondent. His wife answers and then says to her husband, "It's the President."

"Tell him I'm not at home."

She speaks into the phone and then says, "He knows you're at home. You'd better talk to him."

"How does he know?"

"I told you there were two men watching the house before we went to bed."

"Okay. Hello, Mr. President."

"Bob, Ah just want to tell you Ah read your piece on poverty . . ."

"I know it was critical, Mr. President, but . . ."

"Ah thought it was a fine piece, Bob, and you made some very good points. How would you like to join my family?"

"For dinner?"

"No, Bob, my official family. Ah'd like you to be part of the Great Society."

"Well, sir, that's very flattering, but I'm not sure my publishers would want me to . . ."

"Ah spoke to your publisher and he said it's fine with him."

"I don't know what to say, sir. I'd have to think it over."

"Take all the time you want. Ah'll just hang on to the phone here."

"Sir, I don't think I'd do a good job. I've been very hard on the Administration."

"Bob, Ah don't want any yes-men in the Great Society. Your critical approach is what we need. Ah'm not asking you as Lyndon Johnson. Ah'm asking you as President of the United States."

"That's very kind of you, sir. But there are personal considerations."

"Ah understand that. That's why Ah'm not asking you to make up your mind now. Take another thirty seconds."

"I—I—I—just—just don't know what to say, sir."

"Thank you, Bob. The American people will be grateful to you. Bill Moyers will fill you in on what your duties will be."

"Yes, sir, Mr. President. Yes, sir. I'll be there at seven in the morning. Six-thirty? Of course, sir."

The correspondent hangs up the phone. "What am I going to do now?" he asks his wife.

"Leak it?"

"What do you mean, leak it?"

"If you leak the announcement before he does, he won't make the appointment."

The correspondent's eyes fill with tears of gratitude. "Honey, you've done it again."

.

ALL-PURPOSE PRESS RELEASE

Things happen so fast these days that the State Department no longer has time to put out a statement for each crisis. To solve the problem a friend of mine has devised an all-purpose press release which is being sent out to newspapers, magazines and television stations throughout the country.

It goes like this:

DEPARTMENT OF STATE
ALL-PURPOSE PRESS STATEMENT

(Date)

For Release————.

The United States government welcomes the progress, during the past 12 hours, toward freedom and increased stability in ————. While reluctant to condone any resort to violence, we regard the events in ———— as a significant step toward more orderly democracy and the strengthening of the ———— world. We pledge our firm support to Gen. ———— of the ———— party, and are encouraged by his promise to return ———— in due course to civilian rule.

His actions have spelled defeat for the tyrannical forces of (a) General (b) Colonel (c) President (d) Premier (e) Prince ———— of the badly split ———— party, and have given new hope for the free people of ————.

Our support for Gen. ————'s government represents no change in United States policy toward ————.

Nor does it change the United States posture vis-à-vis ———— or ———— or ————.

To help the people of ———— get back on their feet, the President has authorized a special fund of ———— dollars to pay for the salaries of the army and new government officials. The President has also promised ———— dollars in loans to ———— and has promised military aid and advisers to prevent another ————.

The ———— U.S. Fleet has been dispatched to ———— the capital of ———— to prevent further bloodshed and to protect American ———— there.

Secretary of State Dean Rusk denied that the Fleet was sent to ———— to influence in any way the internal affairs of the country. The Fleet had been requested by Gen. ———— and under the ———— agreement we had no choice but to provide American support to prevent a ———— take-over.

Mr. Rusk promised that as soon as things stabilized he would withdraw the ———— Fleet and the ———— Marine Brigade which was landed three days ago.

The President and the National Security Council met today to discuss the ———— situation and the President is sending

—— as his personal representative to give him a firsthand report and to make future recommendations. This in no way shows his lack of confidence in Ambassador ——— ———, who has been called back to Washington for consultation.

Gen. ——— is considered a friend of the United States, having studied at the ——— War College, in Washington, and he has promised strong, forceful leadership for ———, something that has been lacking in the past under the weak regime of ——— and his so-called democratic government.

(a) General (b) Colonel (c) President (d) Premier (e) Prince ——— has sought political asylum in the ——— embassy and will probably be allowed to leave the country.

THE OFFICE OF DENIALS

One of the most important jobs in the government today is to deny a story that has been printed in the press or announced on the radio.

The Special Assistant for Denials in the Johnson Administration is a wispy little man named John J. Categorically, who has an office deep in the bowels of the White House, where he may put out as many as 20 denials in one day.

When I found Mr. Categorically he was just finishing up a denial on a new American military policy. Dictating into a machine, he said, "The United States denies that there has been any shift in its policy on the use of American troops in South Vietnam. American commanders have always had the right to use American troops in combat provided the South Vietnamese forces request them. This is a recorded announcement."

He put down the microphone and said to me, "What can I do for you?"

"Sir, the American people are used to every sort of denial under the Johnson Administration, but nobody knows how your department works. Could you explain it?"

"Well, every morning all the staff members have a meeting and we decide what we're going to announce that day. Then while somebody is working on the announcement I am working on the denial."

"Simultaneously?" I asked.

"Of course. It would be very dangerous to issue a state-

ment without a denial backing it up. The press would never
believe us. Let me give you an example.

"Last week Henry Cabot Lodge, our Ambassador to South
Vietnam, came back to the United States for a meeting with
the President. The White House made the announcement,
and then I drafted a denial that he had returned for any special reason. As soon as the denial was put out, the newspapers realized something important was up, and the story got a
much better play."

"The denial was the key," I said in amazement.

"Exactly."

"Do you always wait for an announcement before you
deny something?"

"Not necessarily. Sometimes we feel it's better to deny an
action just before we do it, more or less to prepare the people
for it. For example, if we're going to send a division of Marines into Vietnam, I will first prepare a denial that such
plans are in the works."

"But what happens when you do send in a Marine division?"

"Then we deny that we ever denied we said we weren't
going to send them. Sometimes the Pentagon will deny a
White House story and sometimes the State Department will
deny a Pentagon story. In this way we're always covered."

"Aren't there ever any slipups?"

"In an operation this big there have to be," he replied.
"We had a heck of a time in the Dominican Republic. First
we had to deny we were supporting either side in the revolution. Then we had to deny we were supporting the rebels.

"Then we had to deny we were supporting the military
junta. Then we had to deny we were violating the OAS
treaty. The UN Ambassador was on the phone to me four-
teen times a day."

"It sounds like a tough business," I said.

"I don't mind it," he said.

Just then a red phone rang and Categorically picked it up.

He took a pencil and started writing. "Yes, sir, you want to
issue a denial that you're annoyed with critics of your foreign
policy. I got it. You welcome differences of opinion. Even
from college professors. No, sir, it's no problem. I'll have it
ready for you in a half hour."

CONFESSIONS OF AN EAVESDROPPER

In 1965 the Senate hearings on electronic eavesdropping and bugging devices reached their high point when it was revealed that you could even record someone's conversation through a martini olive. But the hearings brought back sad memories for me.

I tried to bug someone once.

It was during the days of the McCarthy hearings and the Senator had sent his two young lieutenants, Roy Cohn and David Schine, gumshoeing through Western Europe hoping to find Communists in the State Department.

Cohn and Schine were scheduled to give a press conference in Paris at the American Embassy and I had just purchased for $400 a German wire recorder called a Minephone, which could be hidden in a shoulder holster under your arm. The microphone was an ordinary watch and I was assured I could record anyone's conversation without his knowing it.

I revealed to all my Paris press colleagues that I was armed with this bugging equipment, and I would be able to get everything Cohn and Schine said, as they said it, without their being aware of it. My friends were thrilled and excited. They arranged to have me sit as close to Cohn and Schine as I could get, so each pearl that came from their lips would be recorded.

Then the press proceeded to interrogate the two McCarthy henchmen about their travels. It was a rather hostile press conference, with both sides jabbing and swinging at each other, but it did produce some interesting newsworthy statements from Cohn and Schine.

No one bothered to take any notes, though, because I was recording the conference for everybody.

After the press conference was over, we all rushed to the Crillon Hotel bar, across from the Embassy, and everyone watched excitedly as I took the Minephone out from under my coat and proceeded to play it for the press.

I pressed the "play" button and nothing happened. I checked the batteries and they were in order. I opened the case and suddenly realized what I had done. I was so excited

I had forgotten to turn the recording machine on when the press conference started.

After the first wave of shock hit the correspondents, they went into action. Half the reporters started to try to reconstruct the press conference from memory, while the other half started to beat me over the head with their notebooks.

Bruised and battered, I left the bar in disgrace with the hoots of anger and derision ringing in my ears.

My one big chance to do some bugging for the good of humanity had failed.

But the story does have a happy ending.

Two weeks later, a young man I knew, of wealthy parents, came in to see me. He said he had decided to go in for journalism, and he was wondering if I could give him some advice as to how to go about it.

I thought for a few moments and then I said, "You own a Minephone, I presume."

He didn't even know what it was.

I explained, "If you're going to be a reporter, you've got to have a Minephone. It's a secret recording device that you use for interviews and press conferences."

"Where can I get one?" he asked excitedly.

"They're very hard to come by, but if you come back tomorrow I may be able to find one for you. They cost $400."

"I've got the money," he pleaded. "Please get me one."

The next day I parted with my Minephone and the young man went off toward the Champs-Élysées to start his career in the journalism profession. I don't know how he's made out since, but I wouldn't be in the least surprised to see his name as a winner of the Pulitzer Prize any day now.

THE AGONIZING COLUMNIST

The Vietnamese war has called for some agonizing decisions, but none have been more agonizing than those which have to be made by the Washington political columnists. Although they can seek out the advice of everyone, including the President of the United States, they alone must make the final decision as to what we should do in Southeast Asia.

This burden weighs heavily on each Washington pundit, and every morning, as the people of the world wake up from another fitful night of sleep, they look to the Washington columnists for the solution to the thorny problems that confront us all.

As I walked ino the office of Joseph Wallstop, the widely read syndicated columnist, I saw him silhouetted against the window, bent over a map of the world. I thought to myself how lonely his job must be and how great the risks he must take every day in his column.

He invited me to sit down.

"I'm going to have to call up the reserves tomorrow."

"So soon?" I said.

"I don't see how we can do it any other way. As you know, I was against the peace offensive from the start. I warned the President not to do it. Since he would not take my advice, I see no other choice but to get this country on a war footing."

"But, Mr. Wallstop, the President promised us guns and butter," I pleaded.

"He obviously didn't read my column of October 12, 1965, where I pointed out that the only thing the Communists understood was force.

"To understand this war, you must understand what happened in the Tang dynasty of 987 B.C. The situation was exactly similar except that the Tangs thought they could do business with the Yangs. They found out differently. I hope we're not going to go the way of the Tangs."

"I hope so, too. But how can we avoid it?"

"We must bomb more expensive targets, we must burn bridges and rice fields, oil depots and railroad yards, and we must escalate the escalation. It's all here in my piece of November 26."

"Aren't you afraid of a war with China?"

"Afraid? I'd welcome it. I declared war on China in 1947 and Congress turned me down. Well, the United States pussy-footed for almost twenty years and where did it get us? No one has ever accused me of trying to prevent a war or win a peace."

"Would you advocate using nuclear weapons in South Vietnam?"

"Sparingly. We don't want to win the war and lose the natives. I wouldn't use nuclear weapons against the terrorists in Saigon, for example, but once you get out in the boondocks I think you should use everything you've got."

"Mr. Wallstop, you've advised four Presidents since World War II on how to handle world affairs. How would you say they did?"

"They all let me down sooner or later.

"Under our present form of government, I can only advise a President what to do; I can't make him do it. I believe this is the weakness in our Constitution."

"How do you think President Johnson shapes up compared to others?"

"It's too early to tell yet. If he follows my recommendations, he'll be a great President. If he doesn't, he'll have only himself to blame."

"Suppose he doesn't call up the reserves."

Mr. Wallstop looked at me with his firm jaw jutting out and said, "Then I'll have to call them up myself."

MY TWO YEARS WITH ELAINE

There have been so many stories written by secretaries of famous people that I think it's about time someone wrote a book revealing the intimate details of how it feels to be the boss of a well-known secretary.

My book is entitled *My Two Years With Elaine Narcisso,* or *The First 1,000 Days Dictated But Not Read.*

It begins: "The first time I met Elaine Narcisso was when she came into the office and started cleaning off my desk.

" 'What are you doing that for?' I demanded.

" 'I refuse to work for anybody who keeps papers all over the place,' she said. 'If you want me to work for you, you're going to have to be neat.'

"I promised I would make a big effort.

"Elaine was a fair but tough taskmaster. She was brought up to handle details as well as delegate authority, and although the pressures on her were great, she rarely showed anger. Once I remember, during the 'Bay of Pigs' crisis, I had forgotten to give her a restaurant receipt for a lunch I had had with somebody from the Pentagon, and she flew off the handle and said, 'How am I supposed to keep the books for tax deductions when you don't even save your receipts?'

"I was putting on my shoes and socks at the time and I said, 'I forgot.'

"She broke into tears and as I looked at her I realized that, with all her responsibility and burdens, she was still a very human person.

"Elaine loved to have fun and to tell a good story around the water cooler with her friends, but at the same time when there was work to do she expected the most out of me and hours never counted.

"One summer day I remember deciding to take the day off. I called in to tell her and she said firmly, 'You can't possibly take the day off. You have a meeting with someone from the United Givers Fund, a lunch date with the Malaysian Ambassador, an article to do for the *Ladies Home Journal,* not to mention a term paper you promised a freshman from Syracuse University.'

"I apologized to her for thinking I could take the time off and the incident was forgotten. Elaine was that kind of secretary. She could never stay mad at me for long.

"Occasionally someone would come into the office whom she didn't want me to see and she was very firm about not letting them get through the door. I would always protest that I welcomed any interruption, but she would say, 'First get finished with your column and then we'll talk about whom you can see.'

"Surprisingly, my wife and Elaine got along very well, and what my wife forgot to heckle me about in the morning Elaine would heckle me about in the afternoon. They were always on the phone to each other, my wife asking Elaine to remind me to bring home a sprocket for the lawn mower and my secretary asking my wife to remind me to bring in the manuscript I promised to return to somebody.

"I still have all of Elaine's memos to me and, while I have been offered huge sums to sell them at auction, I think I'll donate them to a library. One says, 'Don't shake hands with your next caller. He thinks it's unclean.' Another says, 'Get rid of her right away. Jock Whitney is in the building.' A third memo says, 'The man you're talking to is not taking a survey. He's really trying to sell you a subscription to *Playboy* magazine.'

"I shall always remember my days working for Elaine Narcisso, as her boss, as the most exciting and challenging days I ever spent in Washington. The hours were long, but the rewards were great, and I learned so much from her that even now I wonder how my life would have been if I couldn't afford a secretary. Different, I'm sure, but then I might never have been able to write this book."

III. PEACE IS HELL

ESCALATION

The American government announced that 1,000 U.S. troops have just landed in South Vietnam. These 5,000 men will be used to protect airfields and vital installations around Saigon, though officials did not rule out that the 15,000 combat-ready soldiers supported by 10,000 aviation personnel would be used to take the fight to the enemy.

An Army spokesman said that the 35,000-troop landing was carried out by plane and sea and that the 50,000-man force, which did not include an armored division, landed earlier in the day, would for the moment constitute enough men to handle the situation. A Defense Department spokesman said:

"If in the near future we discover that these 150,000 men are not enough, we will send in more troops, but it is unlikely, as 200,000 GIs should be sufficient under present fighting conditions."

A newspaperman asked if the sending of 300,000 fresh troops at this time meant that the U.S. "was escalating the war."

"No," he replied, "it means no such thing. We always intended to send in 400,000 troops and this is just part of a military buildup. In a guerrilla war, it is assumed the ratio of troops to the guerrillas is 10 to 1. Since we estimate that there are now 50,000 guerrillas in South Vietnam, our decision to send in 500,000 more soldiers is not unrealistic."

Another reporter asked if the United States intended to get bogged down in a ground war in South Vietnam, something that every American military leader had advised against.

"The answer to your question is negative," the spokesman said. "Our job from the beginning has been to give as much support to the South Vietnamese army as we possibly can. With the arrival of these 700,000 GIs, we can release the South Vietnamese army for major missions."

"Isn't it true that the South Vietnamese government has requested that the American soldiers take over the fighting, while the South Vietnamese regroup and help the people in the villages?"

"There was some talk of that, but the decision will have to be made in Washington. Although we now have 800,000 more American troops, it is still our hope that we can fight side by side with the Vietnamese soldiers."

"Sir, the rumor is that the South Vietnamese army may soon switch roles and become advisers to the American troops."

"The South Vietnamese have offered to cooperate in any way they can. Perhaps at a future date they may take a more active role, but you must remember our latest commitment is only 900,000 men and we have no intention of raising it unless the situation warrants it."

Someone said to the Army spokesman: "Of the 950,000 men landed this morning, how many of them are combat-trained as opposed to service troops?"

"It's hard to say. By the way, gentlemen, I've just been asked to correct the figure I gave you earlier. A million Americans were landed this morning and will be used mostly as an advance force to set up facilities for regular troops who will be landed in the next few weeks."

"How many men will be landed next week?"

"We can't say at this time, but the commitment will be kept to a minimum. While we are pledged to help the South Vietnamese, we don't want to do anything to give the impression that the South Vietnam conflict is an American war."

INDOCTRINATION

The Honolulu meeting was a turning point for the war in Vietnam. President Johnson and Premier Ky spelled out the goals of our commitment there, and these are now being transmitted to our soldiers, sailors, marines, and airmen. But the indoctrination is going rather slowly, and the sergeants are having a hard time explaining the new policy.

"All right, you meat heads. We are now going to discuss why we're fighting in Vietnam. Rosenbloom, why do you think we're fighting in Vietnam?"

"To beat the hell out of the blankety-blank Viet Cong, Sergeant."

"No, Rosenbloom, you're wrong. It's to bring social and economic reforms to the freedom-loving people of South Vietnam. Now, Petrosanni, how will we achieve this goal?"

"By killing every blankety-blank Viet Cong we can find."

"I'm surprised at you, Petrosanni. We will achieve this goal by winning over the natives through public works, education, and good deeds. You had your hand up, Reilly?"

"What do we do with these mortars and flamethrowers?"

"We use them to show the South Vietnamese people that we will not be pushed out by the North Vietnamese. Every time we fire our flamethrowers, we are renewing our pledge to fight oppression, poverty, and disease in Southeast Asia. We can only win this war by getting the confidence of the populace. Now, how do we do this?"

"By bombing the hell out of the towns and villages where the Viet Cong are supposed to be hanging out."

"Exactly, but we must explain to the people why we're bombing their towns and villages. How do we explain it, McPherson?"

"Beats me."

"We explain it by explaining the domino theory. We tell the people that, if South Vietnam falls, then Thailand will fall and then Malaysia and pretty soon all of Southeast Asia will be under the domination of the Communists. What is it, O'Toole?"

"You mean the people won't mind their homes being bombed and their rice fields being burned if we explain it to them afterwards?"

"Right. Once you put people in on the big picture, then their troubles will seem infinitesimal in comparison. Zwacki, you had your hand up."

"Sarge, I would like to know how you tell the good Vietnamese from the bad Vietnamese."

"It's very simple. When you see a native, you yell, 'Nuts to Ho Chi Minh.' If he fires at you, you know he's with the Viet Cong."

"That could be dangerous, Sarge. For example, yesterday Condon got all banged up doing just that. He lost his helmet and his rifle and he wound up in the hospital."

"What happened?"

"Well, he saw this native and he yelled at him, 'Nuts to Ho

Chi Minh,' and the native started firing at him, so Condon fired back.

"Then the Viet Cong guy yelled, 'Nuts to LBJ,' and as Condon and the Viet Cong were shaking hands, a big truck ran over them."

PEACE, ANYONE?

Although there may be a shortage of peace in the world these days, there is certainly no shortage of peacemakers.

President Gamal Abdel Nasser went to Moscow ostensibly to explore the possibilities of peace in Vietnam, where the United States and North Vietnam cannot seem to resolve their differences.

While this is going on, the United States has offered its good offices to help find a peaceful solution to the Kashmir dispute between Pakistan and India. India, which will not give an inch on Kashmir, has indicated it would be willing to act as a mediator in the Malaysian-Indonesian dispute, which has become somewhat touchy of late.

Malaysia, of course, is concerned about the British-Aden controversy, while the British have been hard at work trying to resolve the Turkish-Greek dispute over Cyprus.

The Turks, though ready to attack Greece at any moment, have asked their diplomats to find a peaceful solution to the Iraqi-Kurdistan fighting, and Iraq wants to find some means of settlement of the Sudanese crisis at the very moment the Sudanese have been seeking a way of getting Ethiopia and Somalia to stop attacking each other.

Although Haile Selassie is not about to give way on this thorny problem, he said he was willing to act as mediator in negotiations between the Congo and Brazzaville in their dispute, which has become quite bitter in the last two years.

Meanwhile, back in the Western Hemisphere, Chile is hard at work to find an out to the Dominican Republic crisis, although it has opposed any solution to its border dispute with Bolivia.

President de Gaulle has offered to mediate any dispute anywhere, while refusing to negotiate any kind of nuclear test-ban treaty.

The Soviet Union, while harassing West Berlin, has been

trying behind the scenes to stop Communist China from attacking India.

President Tito keeps traveling around asking heads of state
to reason together while his troops put pressure on the Alban-
ian border.

And while Nasser is in Moscow, American diplomats are
working day and night to talk him out of a war with Israel.

If all this sounds a little ridiculous, the latest word is that
Dr. Martin Luther King, after being hooted out of Los Angeles, now wants to go to Hanoi.

As a matter of fact, you won't find one leader in the world
today who isn't willing to mediate a just peace—for somebody else.

THE CARROT AND THE STICK

President Johnson's "stick and carrot" policy as presented last
April is now being studied by the experts. The stick, we
know, is the bombing of North Vietnam; the carrot he
offered was that if the Communists would stop annoying Saigon, they might expect to get United States aid à la a Southeast Asia Marshall Plan. The man in charge of the stick is
Secretary of Defense McNamara; the man who may be put
in charge of the carrot is Eugene Black, the former head of
the World Bank. I can foresee in the near future where the
interests of these two men could be at odds.

"Bob, this is Gene Black here. I called you about those
railroad bridges you're planning to bomb near Hanoi. I wish
you wouldn't do it, Bob. Railroad bridges cost a lot of money
and as you know the American government is going to have
to eventually pay for them."

"Look, Gene, we've had those railroad bridges targeted for
months. They're the key to Ho's supply lines."

"That's all well and good, Bob, but the Administration has
to answer to Congress for anything you destroy."

"Gene, I think military strategy has to have precedence
over foreign aid."

"Bob, I don't want to be a bore about this, but I have it on
reliable authority that the North Vietnamese want you to
bomb those bridges. They've been hoping to build new ones

for years, but have never been able to get the money. I believe the Defense Department is playing into their hands."

"I resent that, Gene. We've got to keep up the bombing so we can get Hanoi to the negotiation stage. We have to keep up the pressure."

"I'd take issue with you on that. I've already seen the list of things that North Vietnam plans to request as soon as there is a cease-fire. It includes highways, ports, freight trains, trucks, airports and four new Hilton hotels. The more things you wreck, the less reluctant they'll be to call for a cease-fire. They know what happened in Japan and West Germany after the last war, thanks to American bombing, and they have hopes of rebuilding their country in the same way."

"For the moment, Gene, the 'big stick' policy is in effect, and I cannot be concerned with what it will cost us after the war is stopped."

"I'm not asking you to stop the bombing, Bob. All I'm asking you to do is bomb places that have no value, and which they can't justify our rebuilding for them. Is that asking too much?"

"I'll have to talk it over with the Joint Chiefs, but if we don't hurt them we'll never be able to stop the Viet Cong."

"That's another thing I wanted to talk to you about. I wish you'd stop using those fire bombs in South Vietnam. They're terribly destructive and we're going to have to replant all those forests. Couldn't you go back to using nonlethal gas?"

"You're making life very difficult for me, Gene. I believe in foreign aid as much as anybody, but I can't worry about your program. That's the Department of State's problem."

"Okay, go ahead. Wreck their economy and see where it gets us. We've only got a billion dollars to play with, and if you keep up your bombing attacks, I'm going to have to cut South Vietnam out of our program."

THE NEW ARMY

The Chief of Staff of the Army, Gen. Harold K. Johnson, circulated an order telling Army drill sergeants to clean up their language. In other words, no more swearing at recruits. The order came as a shock to most Army NCOs, whose vocabulary of four-letter words had been their only source of communication. Some sergeants were so thrown by the order that they haven't been able to utter a sound since.

But the military can adapt to any situation and many drill sergeants got into the spirit of the new regulation.

One day I attended a training camp where the order had just gone into effect.

The drill sergeant came into the barracks at six in the morning and shouted, "Wakey, wakey, everyone! It's a glorious morning and you're all invited out on the veranda to join me for exercises."

"Say, Sarge," one of the privates said, "I'm tired. Do you mind if I sleep this morning?"

"Why not, Wozinski? It's your Army. Could you meet us at the rifle range when you're in the mood?"

"I'll try," the private said, "but I'm not making any promise."

"That's a good boy, Wozinski. Now, everybody out on the veranda."

Only half the platoon was dressed. The other half had stayed in their sacks.

The sergeant seemed pleased. "Well, we have more than enough to start with. I have a surprise for you men. We're going to march over to the mess hall together and I'm going to count cadence."

The platoon started catcalling and booing.

"Now, come on, fellows. That's not nice. After all, I'm your drill sergeant. Why don't we try it? If you don't like it, we won't do it again."

The men shrugged their shoulders and started marching toward the mess hall.

"Smith and O'Malley," the sergeant said, "you're out of step."

"Out of step with what?" O'Malley wanted to know.

"The rest of the platoon."

"That's no way to talk to a recruit," Smith said. "We're doing the best we can."

"We've only got two feet," O'Malley shouted.

"I'm sorry," the sergeant said. "Forget I brought it up."

"Okay, but don't forget we're human too," Smith muttered.

Later in the morning the drill sergeant held inspection in the barracks.

"Barstow," he said, "why didn't you make up your bed this morning?"

"I forgot."

"Suppose everyone in the Army forgot, Barstow? Then we'd all be living like pigs."

"Look," said Barstow, "a guy's got a right to make a mistake once in a while. I made it up yesterday morning, didn't I?"

"I suppose you're right, Barstow. Do you want me to make the bed for you today?"

"Suit yourself, since it bothers you and it doesn't bother me."

In the afternoon the sergeant announced the platoon would go on a hike. He ordered full packs, rifles, and cartridge belts.

Three of the recruits drove up in station wagons.

"What are you fellows doing?" the sergeant asked.

"What's the matter," one of the recruits said, "you never heard of Hertz rent-a-car?"

"Oh, damn," the sergeant said.

Just then an officer walked by. "Sergeant, did I hear you curse?"

"I was just muttering."

"It came out loud and clear. Let's go over and talk to the C.O. about this."

HOW TO BE DRAFTED

There have been so many articles and pamphlets written on "How to Avoid the Draft," that it is only right someone should put out instructions on "How to Be Drafted." I know I'll be criticized for this, but under the American system a person has as much right to be drafted as he does to avoid it.

THE FIRST THING TO DO

Notify your draft board that you are ready to go immediately and tell them you want to leave in the next draft call. They will probably turn your case over to the local psychiatrist in your district.

MEETING WITH
THE PSYCHIATRIST

Tell the psychiatrist that you are eager to get into uniform and your only hope is that as soon as you've finished basic training they'll send you to Vietnam. If he asks you why you want to go, tell him you believe it's your patriotic duty to defend your flag and country. You want to protect your home, your mother and the unborn millions of American children against the specter of godless Communism.

He will undoubtedly declare you 4-F on the grounds that anyone who is so eager to get into the Army is nuts.

YOU HAVE A RIGHT
TO APPEAL

Write to General Hershey of the Selective Service in Washington, D.C., and give him the facts. Tell him your draft board has been scheming to prevent you from going into the Army. Imply that the psychiatrist who examined you had it in for you because you wanted to fight for your country.

Insist that General Hershey sign your orders himself, which will make it possible for you to go into the service immediately.

He will turn your letter over to the FBI to see if there is any Communism mixed up in your psychiatric background.

WHEN THE FBI COMES TO VISIT YOUR HOME

You have a right to answer any question the FBI asks you. They may insist that you take the Fifth Amendment so you can be listed as a security risk. But stand on your Constitutional grounds and reply to their questions. If they ask you why you want to be drafted, tell them you're sick and tired of reading about guys burning up their draft cards and pretending they're homosexuals just to get out of the service.

Show respect to the agents and say "sir" to them. Tell them you have always admired the FBI and ask them if they can get you an autographed picture of J. Edgar Hoover. The more forthright you are, the more suspicious they'll get. When they discover you've never joined any left-wing organizations, they'll know something is fishy and from then on they'll keep a close eye on you.

YOU CAN ALWAYS PICKET

When things look black, you can picket the Pentagon, demanding that Secretary McNamara overrule your local draft board and draft you into the service. If need be, lie down in front of a troop train taking draftees to camp and urge the troop commander to take you on board.

You will probably be locked up, but at least you will have made your point.

WHEN ALL ELSE FAILS

Announce to the newspapers that you have no intention of being drafted and that you are against the war in Vietnam. The draft board will take you immediately and the Army will make a soldier of you overnight.

TROUBLE WITH ESCALATION

The trouble when you escalate a war is that you not only have to escalate the troops but also the VIPs who want to visit the area where you're fighting.

In the beginning, when we first started helping out in South Vietnam, our policy was to keep our VIPs to a minimum, on the theory that it was a South Vietnamese war and our VIPs should act in an advisory capacity only.

But as the succeeding South Vietnamese governments kept knocking off their own VIPs in military coups, we had no choice but to replace them with American VIPs who soon were being escorted all over the country.

For a long time, the Department of Defense refused to discuss how many VIPs they intended to send to Vietnam. The reason they gave is that it took five American soldiers to protect one American VIP, and if they revealed how many VIPs intended to go to Vietnam, the enemy would know how many soldiers we planned to send there.

But then President Johnson announced he was going to send 140,000 American troops to protect our position in Southeast Asia. This meant we could expect 28,000 VIPs to visit "our" boys.

Unfortunately, more VIPs requested to go to Saigon, and so we had to up our commitment to 165,000 troops.

If the rate of VIP visits goes up, which it shows every intention of doing, we may soon have between 600,000 and 700,000 American GIs in Vietnam.

This is the main trouble with escalation. The more troops you throw in, the more VIPs want to visit the place, and then you have to send in more troops to protect them.

It's not just a question of Congressmen and Senators going to Vietnam. You also have Defense Department officials, leading businessmen, Broadway shows, Hollywood movie stars, syndicated columnists, magazine publishers, television network executives, baseball players, clergy, and psychological warfare experts.

Though it is not generally known, one of the conditions that the North Vietnamese have made for negotiations is that although the American troops can stay in Vietnam, the VIPs would have to pull out. The Americans stationed in Vietnam are happily willing to give in on this point, although Washington has turned it down repeatedly. Without VIPs, Washington maintains, no one would know what a wonderful job we're doing over there and morale on the home front would collapse.

There was a time when VIPs were just willing to visit a few bars in Saigon, then return to the United States. But now most VIPs insist on helicopter flights over enemy territory and hazardous visits to Special Forces camps. This has produced a great strain on the military equipment, but it has given the Armed Forces a chance to check out new methods of handling VIPs.

Many new techniques have been innovated which were unheard of in World War II and the Korean conflicts.

For one thing, the new type of VIP wants to see the war for himself, and although he would like to be shot at, he certainly doesn't want to get hit. This has put the military on its toes.

It is rumored that some VIPs are flown over friendly territory and shot at by our own troops, but this has been vehemently denied by the Defense Department.

There is a Pentagon order that no GI may fire at an American VIP no matter how much he is provoked. But in Vietnam, as we all know, anything can happen and usually does.

THE PEACE FEELERS

One of the trickiest things to recognize in Washington are legitimate "peace feelers" from the enemy. In a *Look* magazine article Eric Sevareid wrote that Adlai Stevenson had told him the United States rejected a "peace feeler" from Hanoi through UN Secretary-General U Thant in August of 1964. The State Department confirmed that the offer had been made, but thanks to Dean Rusk's antenna, which is very sensitive to peace feelers, the U.S. had turned it down.

The Assistant Secretary for Peace Feelers in the State Department told me one day, "I don't know what all the fuss is about. We've had a lot of peace feelers from the Commies, but not one of them has shown up on Dean Rusk's feeler set as being legitimate."

"How do you know when a peace feeler is legitimate or not?" I asked.

"We have a peace-feeler evaluator here," he said, taking me over to what looked like a very complicated radio set. "When a peace feeler comes in, we broadcast to Dean Rusk, who picks it up on his counter-peace feeler. This feeler, attached to the Secretary's head, is so sensitive that it can tell within seconds whether it is a sincere feeler or just another lousy Communist trick."

"Could you demonstrate it for me?"

"Well, I don't know if the Secretary has his counterfeeler on his head now or not. Let's try it." He spoke into the machine. "Hanoi told Bulgaria it will meet with American representatives in Geneva."

There was crackling static and finally a weak voice came over which said, "Turn the offer down."

The Assistant Secretary switched the machine off.

"That's marvelous," I said. "It's almost like extrasensory perception."

"It's the greatest breakthrough we've had since radar," he said proudly.

"Would it work for any Secretary of State?" I asked.

"We don't know. Dean Rusk's feeler is his own. We just built the machinery to fit it."

"Is this the only way you people handle peace feelers?" I asked.

"Oh, no. For the time being it's the most foolproof, but we have other methods as well. Timing is very important when it comes to peace feelers. For example, when you're losing a war, you've got to ignore them or the other side will get you in a box. The peace feeler from them may be legitimate, but you certainly don't want to take it up with people committing naked aggression."

"Then you would only take up a peace feeler when you're winning?" I said.

"No, not necessarily. When you're winning there is no reason to sit down and talk peace because then you might have to work out a compromise with the naked aggressors."

"But if you can't accept a peace feeler when you're losing and you can't accept one when you're winning, when can you accept one?"

"If I told you that I'd be giving aid and comfort to the enemy."

"Do you ever send out peace feelers of your own?"

"All the time. The President has said he will talk peace anywhere, anytime, with no conditions attached."

"Have they ever picked up your feelers?"

"As far as we know they haven't."

"Why not?"

"We don't know, unless it's because they've got one of these damn feeler machines of their own."

A NEW PEACE PLAN

Men of goodwill everywhere are trying to find a just solution to the Vietnam problem. Many peace plans have been proposed. The latest comes from my good friend N. K. Hopkins, who lives in Chaumont, France.

Hopkins points out that the 1954 Geneva agreements call for free elections in both halves of Vietnam. The elections were to decide whether the South should go Ho or remain Nhu and whether the North should stay Ho or go go.

For some reason the elections were never held.

Now one of Ho's conditions for a peace settlement is to initiate the 1954 Geneva agreements. It is time, Hopkins believes, to take him up on it.

The next time Ho screams for elections we should agree. The only thing we must insist on though is that there be complete freedom of ballot.

Of course, in the elections, we would lose South Vietnam. We knew all along we would.

But we would win in the North. The people who have been living under Ho would certainly vote him out in an honest election, just as the people in the South would figure anything they got would be better than what they have now.

Therefore, Ho would move his government to Saigon and General Westmoreland, his troops, and the current South Vietnamese Premier would go to Hanoi.

What Ho would inherit in the South would be refugees, religious strife, and a war-torn economy.

While we, on the other hand, in the North would get an industrialized, underpopulated, de-viced, and thoroughly pacified country.

Not only that, but in North Vietnam we would be virtually surrounded by Communist countries, so we could easily make it into a showcase for capitalism and a bastion for democracy. North Vietnam would be a new symbol for the free world.

Besides, we would have a border near the heart of China, which would make our espionage easier, and Hanoi could become a new listening post for the West. And with North Vietnam as a base, Chiang Kai-shek's return to the mainland would be that much nearer.

Ho, on the other hand, would find himself with millions of unemployed guerrillas which he would try to send North. But the people in the North know what it is to live under Ho, so they would reject them. The guerrillas would then return to Saigon to demand pensions and land. But the Southern economy wouldn't be able to take it, so the guerrillas would revolt against Ho, and we would support them, sending supplies and advisers along the newly opened LBJ Trail.

If everything goes according to the script, Ho would soon ask us to take over South Vietnam again, something we would refuse to do.

Ho would then become furious with China for advising him in the first place to agree to the elections, and he would throw in his lot with the Russians who could not refuse to give him financial assistance. But the cost of rebuilding the South would be so great that the Soviets would find themselves in an economic crisis, and they would have to postpone their timetable for a Communist takeover of the world.

Thus, we would kill three birds with one stone. And Cabot Lodge could then come home.

PEACE IS HELL

As the Johnson peace offensive goes into its third year, more and more attention is being paid to responses from Hanoi. Everyone is looking for some sort of sign that North Vietnam is ready to come to the negotiating table, and every reply to our peace overtures is studied by our experts in minute detail.

Therefore, what might sound on the surface like a complete rejection of an offer could very well be the opening we've been looking for.

I went over to the State Department the other day and talked to a U.S. Hanoi-watcher, who was, at that very moment, studying the latest North Vietnam radio broadcast concerning our peace offensive.

"It looks promising," he said, as he shoved his magnifying glass to one side.

"How's that?" I asked.

"Well, listen to this," he continued, reading from the report. "The U.S. policy of aggression in Vietnam remains unchanged and shows the arrogance of President Johnson in pretending he wants peace while American and puppet troops intensify their attacks on innocent women and children."

"That's promising?" I said.

"It's a very mild statement compared to the one they made last week."

"What else did they say?"

"U.S. imperialists will be thrown into the sea long before any peace swindle can be made, and their lackeys in Saigon will be chewed up by the democratic peoples of Vietnam."

"That sounds bad," I said.

"On the contrary, there's a great glimmer of hope here. This is the first time Hanoi has mentioned the sea. It may have significance. It's quite possible they might want to negotiate on water rather than land."

"That's something I hadn't thought of."

"Now here, in the third paragraph, may be another hint that they're ready to talk. It says, 'North Vietnam will never be blackmailed into giving away the rights of the National Front for Liberation by a nation who sabotaged the 1954 Geneva agreements, and who have shamelessly launched air attacks on the cities and villages, leaving behind wanton destruction and horror.' "

"What kind of hint do you get out of that?" I asked.

"This is the first time they've mentioned the Geneva agreements in a broadcast, and its quite possible this is their way of telling us, without the Chinese knowing, of course, that they would be willing to go there."

"By George, you may be right," I said excitedly.

"Now down here in the broadcast they make their usual attacks on our imperialism and credibility. Then they say, 'There is no possible way of ever negotiating peace in Vietnam until every American soldier leaves this country.' "

"That's a tough statement," I said.

"We've asked them to clarify it. You'll note they don't say when the soldiers should leave. There could be two meanings to it. Possibly three.

"Here, at the end, they say, 'So long as U.S. imperialists still pursue the war of aggression against Vietnam and launch attacks against the fatherland, the people in both zones of Vietnam will fulfill their sacred duty to resist with the aid of their peace-loving friends in China and the Soviet Union. Let them make no mistake about this.' "

"It sounds like a peace feeler to me," I said.

"We're treating it like that, until we get word to the contrary."

WAR IS WHAT?

Every war deserves a war movie and the Vietnamese war is no exception. Hollywood has been in a race to see which company will come out with its picture first. But everyone is bogged down with plot troubles.

This story conference at Zenith Studios will give you some idea of what the film makers are up against.

"All right," the head of the studio says. "What's going on with the Vietnam movie?"

"Well, sir, we're having a little trouble. The American part of the picture is no problem. We have a part for John Wayne, as the tough paratrooper Colonel, Frank Sinatra as the free-wheeling salty Sergeant and Sal Mineo as the kid who has never been tested under fire. But we're in difficulty with the enemy."

"Why?"

"Well, no one knows how to tell the South Vietnamese from the South Viet Cong. They all look alike."

"Why didn't you ask the Defense Department?"

"We did, and they don't know either."

The studio head thinks a minute. "Why don't we show the Viet Cong looking sneaky and menacing and the South Vietnamese looking friendly and always smiling?"

"That's the problem," one of the writers says. "Our research indicates the Viet Cong are always smiling and looking friendly whenever you see them. That's why they're so dangerous."

"Okay then, let's make the good Vietnamese look sneaky and menacing and the bad Vietnamese look friendly and smiling."

"If we do that, we don't get any cooperation from the South Vietnamese government."

"What government?"

"The one that's in when we make the picture."

"Why do we have to have cooperation from the South Vietnamese government in the first place? Why can't we make the picture here in Hollywood?"

"Because we can't find enough Vietnamese extras."

The studio head says, "Use Japanese."

"Okay, even if we resolve that problem, we still have the story to worry about. In our script John Wayne, Frank Sinatra and Sal Mineo are attacking a village where some Viet Cong are hiding out."

"It sounds logical."

"The Defense Department is against it. They say they don't want to show American soldiers attacking a South Vietnamese village because the Americans are in South Vietnam to protect the villagers and not attack them. We had a great scene when the paratroopers couldn't find any Viet Cong, so they burned every straw hut to the ground.

"But the Defense Department nixed it. They say they want us to show the paratroopers rebuilding a village that the Viet Cong burned down."

The studio head muses, "If we can't see the Viet Cong and we can't attack a target in force and we can't tell the difference between the good guys and the bad guys, why are we making the picture at all?"

"To show the Communist world that we're not going to be kicked out of South Vietnam."

"How do we do that?"

"Well, in one scene we had written, Sinatra tells his Vietnamese girl friend, Nancy Kwan, why the Americans are there, but the Defense Department didn't like it."

"Why not?"

"The American GIs aren't allowed to fraternize with Vietnamese women."

"What the hell kind of war film is that?" the studio head shouts.

"That's what I said and Defense said, if they have to fight a different kind of war we should be willing to make a different kind of war picture."

THE BATMAN COMETH

"When all else fails, the President of the United States still has one secret weapon which he and he alone has the power to use. One night last week, when all else failed, the President decided to use it."

Lights up—we see phone and hear ringing.

Suddenly Batman comes out on stage and walks over to the phone. He picks it up. "Yes, chief. You want to speak to Valenti? He's in the Batroom. . . . Just a minute. I'll get him."

Jack Valenti, dressed as Robin, comes out on stage.

"Hello, chief, this is Robin. Robin Valenti. Yes, I know—I changed my name to Robin so Marvin Watson wouldn't be able to trace my telephone calls. . . . What's that? Holy Fulbright! You'd better speak to the Batman." As he hands the phone to Batman, he says, "He wants us to go to Vietnam."

The Batman grabs the phone and says to Robin, "He must be out of his mind." Then he speaks into the phone, "Yes, chief; but chief . . . ; yes, I know, chief. . . . But I'm 4-F. I've got psychological problems. Why else would I be wearing leotards?"

Robin: "Tell him I've got a bad knee."

Batman: "Robin has a bad knee. Why don't you send Cassius Clay?"

The Batman hangs up. Turns to Robin. "He says if we don't go, he'll get us on income taxes."

Robin: "Holy J. Edgar Hoover! He must know about the money we kept from the Brink's robbery."

"Well, Robin, we better see what the computer says."

They go over to the computer.

Batman says, "If your name was Ho, where would you go?"

Robin: "Ho—go—I would go to Hanoi. But it doesn't rhyme."

Batman: "Good thinking, Boy Wonder. That's how Ho has fooled everyone. Now if you played a gong, where would it clong?"

Robin: "In the Viet Cong!"

Batman: "Robin, I think Ho is behind the Viet Cong."

Robin: "Holy McNamara! We better tell Dean Rusk."

Batman: "Wait, Robin. Rusk has enough problems as it is. We'd better take care of Ho ourselves."

Robin: "But how?"

Batman: "Let's see what the computer says."

Batman takes out card.

Robin: "What does it say?"

Batman: *"By all means, escalate."*

Robin: "Holy Joe Alsop! Look, there's another card."

Batman takes second card. *"Get out of Vietnam."*

Robin: "Holy Walter Lippmann! There's a third card."

Batman reads third card. *"Bomb Hanoi."*

Robin says: "Holy Goldwater!"

Batman reads fourth card. *"Take it to the United Nations."*

Robin: "Holy Goldberg!"

Batman: "We're in trouble, Robin. I'm not about to go to Vietnam. I was a veteran in World War II."

Robin: "And I'm not about to go to Vietnam. I went to the University of California at Berkeley."

Batman: "But how can we get out of it?"

Robin: "Holy Bill Moyers! I think I've got it. If we announce the President is sending us to Vietnam before he announces it, he'll get so mad he won't send us."

Batman: "Robin, that's good thinking. What's Drew Pearson's telephone number?"

CRACK TROOPS OF NONOMURA

As you probably remember, the country of South Nonomura has been fighting the Communist guerrillas for four years. Thanks to American military aid and American advisers, South Nonomura now has one of the best-equipped armies in the world, and when it comes to hardware the South Nonomuran soldier lacks nothing. Newsreels of the crack South Nonomuran troops show them flying off into the jungle in American helicopters, armed to the teeth. You get a feeling of pride that a group of peasants like the South Nonomurans can be whipped into a first-class fighting outfit.

Unfortunately, despite all the aid, the South Nonomurans haven't been doing very well against the North Nonomuran guerrillas, who are armed with nothing more than fishing rods and World War II rifles. Why, everyone asks, can't the South Nonomuran army contain the guerrillas?

One of our correspondents came back after an interview with a crack South Nonomuran officer and showed us his notes. The interview shed some light on the problem.

CORRESPONDENT: Captain, how is the war going?

CAPTAIN: War going great. Tell Americans we like K-rations very much, but Q-rations lousy. We need more cigarettes and beer. Morale very low without beer.

CORRESPONDENT: Why hasn't your army been able to contain the guerrillas?

CAPTAIN: Our army trained by Americans to fight enemy in open. Lousy Communists hide in jungle.

CORRESPONDENT: Why don't you go into the jungle and get them?

CAPTAIN: You crazy or something? You can get bitten by snakes in the jungle. Besides, your uniform gets dirty. We have to keep uniforms nice and clean for coup d'état.

CORRESPONDENT: That's true.

CAPTAIN: And don't forget, you have to walk in jungle. Since Americans came, my men won't go anywhere unless it's by truck or helicopter. Walking is for lousy Communists.

CORRESPONDENT: There have been many instances where you

have had the Communists surrounded and they've disappeared. How do you explain this?

CAPTAIN: Very simple. As soon as we hear about lousy Communist attack, we send crack soldiers there to fight them. But crack soldiers must be supported by many men. We must have hot food, showers, officers' club, noncommissioned officers' club, PX, chaplain, movies and comfortable living quarters. By the time my crack outfit is ready to fight, lousy Communists have escaped into jungle.

CORRESPONDENT: Wouldn't it be better if you fought the war without all these things?

CAPTAIN: We crack outfit. Thanks to American training and know-how we not going to fight dirty war like dirty Communists.

CORRESPONDENT: But you're not getting anywhere.

CAPTAIN: That's what you think. In another year I make colonel. Then I overthrow the government. You see me then, I give you good interview.

CORRESPONDENT: But, Captain, isn't there some way of turning the tide against the guerrillas?

CAPTAIN: It's too late. My crack troops have taste of American way of life. We are so busy keeping them supplied, we don't have much time to fight lousy Communists. All they talk about these days is GI Bill of Rights.

CORRESPONDENT: Is there anything you need that would help speed up the war?

CAPTAIN: Yes, send us more Japs.

CORRESPONDENT: Japs?

CAPTAIN: You know, Jap transistor radios.

STOCK MARKET JITTERS

MARKET PLUMMETS IN LATE SELLING WAVE—STOCK MARKET JITTERS CAUSED BY WAR SCARE. Every time there is a war crisis in the United States one of the first reactions seems to be from Wall Street. Why people sell their stocks when they think that there may be a chance of a war is something that nobody has been able to figure out.

It makes you wonder what it will be like after WW III. We're in a fallout shelter 150 feet below the earth. Above the ground as far as the eye can see is nothing but rubble.

The few survivors in the shelter have to remain underground for at least three weeks until the radioactivity blows away.

The first man says, "Well, it could have been worse. I managed to sell my Xerox at 113 the day before the war started."

The second man says, "You did a smart thing. I held on to mine, and I don't know what it's worth now."

The first man says, "I've always been bearish about war. I know it's supposed to help the economy and all that, but when I started reading those scare headlines, I said, 'Stanley, it's time to get out of the market.' "

The second man says, "You mean you sold all your stocks?"

"Yup, my broker was against it, but I said I'm getting out."

"What did you put your money in?"

"Tax-free municipal bonds."

A third man says, "I was lucky, too. I sold my General Motors at 97¼ and my Comsat at 64½, about three hours before the attack came. My portfolio should be in pretty good shape when I get out of here."

The fourth man says, "An hour before I came down here I got a call for more margin on my Hilton Hotels. I tried to borrow some money, but all the banks had closed, so I think I'm wiped out. I guess I wouldn't have minded it, except my broker was so nasty to me over the phone."

The third man says, "I wouldn't probably have sold at all except I subscribe to a financial newsletter and they had a short article last week by an economist who said that in case of an all-out atomic attack there would probably be a break in the Dow Jones averages. The guy made sense."

"My newsletter said just the opposite," the second man says. "It pointed out that inflation would probably set in after another war and advised its subscribers to buy as many blue chips as possible."

"The patriotic thing, of course, in times like this is to buy government bonds," the third man says.

"But the bond market has been soft," the fourth man says. "I was told the one thing people would want after a catastrophe like this would be entertainment, so I took a heavy position in Warner Brothers, MGM, and Universal Pictures."

The first man says, "I don't know what it's like up there now, but my guess is that it would be a good time to buy American Tel & Tel. There's going to be a lot of telephoning once this thing is over."

The second man says, "Since there are only four of us down here together, I'd like to pass on a little tip I got from the chairman of the board of Zing Electronics. He said as soon as the all-clear is sounded he's going to announce a three-for-one split of the stock."

The other three look at him. The first man says, "How many other people know about this?"

"As far as I know, just the chairman and the four of us."

"Let's go up and start buying right away."

The other three are on their feet.

The fourth man says, "This is what I call being in the right place at the right time."

IV. THE DESEGREGATED BULL

THE DESEGREGATED BULL

Every once in a while a glimmer of light shines through the darkness of segregation in Alabama. Recently an Aberdeen Angus bull, which was bought for the record price of $176,400, was operated on to restore his virility. The operation was performed at Auburn University in Alabama in hopes that the bull, whose name is Lindertis Evulse, would be able to serve his functon as a mate to 10,000 cows a year. By artificial insemination, of course.

While everybody is awaiting the results, the state of Alabama's House of Representatives and Senate have both passed resolutions wishing Lindertis Evulse a speedy recovery and a long and happily prolific life. The most amazing thing about the resolution—and the thing the Alabama legislature overlooked—was that Lindertis Evulse is a black bull.

This raises some interesting questions. It is assumed that if the operation is a success Lindertis Evulse will be mated with cows of other colors—some even white, and this certainly will not serve the cause of segregation.

Another is that if Lindertis Evulse makes it at the University of Auburn many black bulls from all over the world will apply for admission and it will be impossible for educational officials to turn them down on the grounds of creed or color.

It may be the first big breakthrough in Alabama for better race relations.

This is not to say there are not many stumbling blocks.

One of the reasons bulls have not wanted to go to an Alabama university is that they've seen what the authorities down there can do with cattle prods.

While it is true that the prods so far have only been used on people, it is possible that some overzealous police chief might decide to use them on cattle.

Also, if the black bulls are too successful, they may start taking stud fees away from the white bulls, and this could cause a tremendous amount of friction on the range.

Another problem is housing. If you put a black bull in a white barn, there will be a great cry of protest from the parents of cows who fear for the safety of their offspring.

Then there is the question of what happens in a restaurant in Alabama. Is it proper for a steak fathered by a black bull to be served in an all-white restaurant? If so, should the steak be labeled so the customer can refuse it and ask for a steak from an all-white bull, if he is so inclined?

These are only a few of the problems that have been raised since Lindertis Evulse was admitted to Auburn. They can't be solved overnight, but everyone is optimistic. If the Alabama legislature can pass a resolution in favor of a black bull, it may someday pass one in favor of a black person.

In the meantime, everyone is rooting that Lindertis Evulse's operation turns out successfully and he will be all bull again.

If it works out the way the medical people at Auburn hope it will, Alabamans will then have to ask each other, "Would you want your cow to marry a black Aberdeen Angus?"

ALABAMA LITERACY TEST

Getting to vote in Bull Whip, Ala., isn't as easy as one would think. First, you have to sneak around a mounted sheriff's posse, then fight your way through a cloud of state police tear gas, and then you have to leap over a hundred cattle prods. And finally, if you still want to vote in Bull Whip, you have to register, and the registration office in the courthouse is open only from 11:55 P.M. to midnight on every sixth Saturday of the month.

The problem is that, although the registration office is open, the courthouse is closed, and it's kind of hard to get into the building.

Even so, Mr. George Abernathy, a Negro, manages, much to the surprise of the registrar, to get in and asks to register to vote.

"Fine, George, fine. Ah'd be glad to register you as soon as you answer a few of these here questions," the registrar says. "Now, first off, what is your educational background?"

"I was a Rhodes scholar, I received a B.A. from Columbia, a masters from Harvard, and a Ph.D. from MIT."

"That's just fine, George. Now let me ask you this. Can you read an' write?"

"I've written three books, on cybernetics, Christian philosophy, and advanced political theory."

"Ah'd appreciate it if you didn't use such big words, George. If there's anything Ah hate it's an uppity voter."

Abernathy says, "I believe I have a right to register."

"Yes, you do, George, but I have to give you this here literacy test 'cause we cain't have ignoramuses voting for our great Governor, George Wallace, if you know what Ah mean. Now, first off, would you please read somethin' from this here newspaper?"

"It's in Chinese."

"That's right."

Abernathy reads three stories from the Chinese paper. The registrar is thrown, but he doesn't want to show it.

"All right, now will you read the hieroglyphics off this here Rosetta Stone?" he says.

Mr. Abernathy reads the hieroglyphics and the registrar begins to get nervous.

"George, here is the constitution of Finland, in Finnish. Would you please interpret the first 14 articles for me?"

"What has that got to do with voting in Alabama?"

"We got to keep out agitators and the like. Now, you going to take the test or not?"

Mr. Abernathy interprets the 14 articles and the registrar becomes truly frightened. He telephones the Governor's office and reports what is happening. An aide comes back in a few minutes and says, "The Governor says to give him Part 4 of the test."

The registrar goes to his safe and takes out a clay jar. "George, there's only one more thing you're obligated to do for this here literacy test. Would you be so kind as to read for me any two of these Dead Sea Scrolls?"

Mr. Abernathy reads the first one but stumbles on a word in the second one.

"Ah'm sorry, George. You've failed the literacy test, but you can come back next year and try again."

As Abernathy leaves the office, a white Alabaman comes in to register to vote.

The registrar says to him, "Would you please spell cat for me?"

The white voter says, "K-A-T."

"Try it again. You're getting warm."

THE TRIAL OF JACK THE RIPPER

After reading the accounts of the trial in Haynesville, Alabama, where a jury found a socially prominent citizen "not guilty" of killing a civil rights seminary student, one wonders how Jack the Ripper would have fared if he had been a citizen of Alabama and had been caught and tried in Lowndes County.

It might have gone something like this:

First, the grand jury would indict him for manslaughter instead of murder on the grounds that, although he killed five women, it was done without malice.

Then the trial takes place. An all-white jury made up of friends of the Ripper family is selected, and the judge, who is Jack's uncle, warns the prosecution to be brief and refrain from calling too many witnesses.

The county prosecutor reluctantly charges that Jack killed five women by slitting their throats and spreading their innards about. The people in the courtroom chuckle and several of Jack's cousins wave to him. The prosecutor produces the knife as evidence and then rests his case.

The defense attorney for Jack does not deny the charges, which causes members of the KKK in the courtroom to applaud. But he maintains Jack was acting in self-defense.

He calls his first witness. "Did you see the defendant stab his first victim?"

"Yes, sir, I did. Rip was walking down the street late at night when this here woman pulls a switchblade on him, and he had no choice but to slash out at her first. It was quick thinking on his part, because that woman meant to do him harm."

The second witness, Zeke Ripper, is called.

"Zeke, eight days after Rip defended himself, he ran into another woman on the street. What was her name?"

"Dark Annie Chapman."

"Would you repeat that again?"

"Dark Annie Chapman."

"What happened, Zeke?"

"Wal, Rip is just strolling along and suddenly Dark Annie comes up to him with a pistol in her hand like she's going to kill him, so Jack pulls out his knife and slits her throat."

"Where's the pistol now, Zeke?"

"Some nigra rushed up and took it away 'fore the police came."

"Thank you, Zeke. Now, ladies and gentlemen of the jury, I'm not even going to call any witnesses in regards to the killings of 'Long Liz' Stride and Kate Edowes, because there is no need to. Jack saw both these women kissing nigras and he went up to them and told them to stop it and when they didn't Jack did what any Haynesville gentleman would do and stabbed them both in the abdomen.

"As for the killing of Black Mary Kelly, I'd like to call Jefferson Lingo Ripper. Jefferson, what happened, in your own words?"

"This here Black Mary, she comes up to Rip and she said something to him that I can't repeat here in court and poor Rip followed her to her room and cut her up. I've known Rip since he was a boy and he wouldn't hurt a fly, but that woman provoked him something awful."

Laughter from the court.

"Are these Black Mary's clothes?"

"Yes, sir."

"Ladies and gentlemen of the jury, I ask you, what kind of woman would wear clothes like this and bring shame and world-wide publicity to the good people of Lowndes County? No white man will be safe on the streets of Hayneville if you find Jack the Ripper guilty of defending himself. Put yourself in his place. Wouldn't you have done the same thing?"

The judge asks the jury to file out and decide a verdict.

The foreman says, "No need for that, Judge. We find the defendant not guilty and we wish to take this opportunity to nominate Jack the Ripper for sheriff of this God-fearing community."

WHITE HOUSE SIT-IN

There was a great deal of criticism about the sit-in at the White House last March, not only from the people who represent law and order in this country, but also from other sit-ins who were pretty mad about it.

"The discouraging thing," a bearded fellow who was sitting in front of the Department of Justice parking lot told me, "is those people who sat in at the White House were youngsters without any sit-in experience at all. The White House has always been considered the Mt. Everest for sit-ins, an unattainable goal which we aspired to only in our wildest dreams.

"Most of us have come up through the ranks, some sitting down on campuses, others in restaurants, others in front of courthouses. But these kids, none over the age of twenty-one, decided to sit in the White House.

"What do they have to look forward to after that? I think they made a mistake. They'll be ruined for life. They can only go down from there."

"You're not jealous of them, are you?" I asked him.

"Jealousy has nothing to do with it. But there were so many more sit-ins deserving of the honor—veterans of the University of California disturbances, Ban-the-Bomb demonstrations, and World's Fair sit-ins—that it doesn't seem right that these kids should have been allowed to sit at the White House."

"Perhaps it was just a spur-of-the-moment thing," I said. "Maybe they hadn't planned on sitting there until they got in. You can get pretty tired waiting in line to go through the White House."

"I believe it was planned. I think those kids just took the law into their own hands without consulting the rest of us. They're like American kids everywhere, impatient and impulsive. They figure why should they sit on cold pavements in the rain like the rest of us? They're spoiled. They've had everything handed to them on a silver platter. They never sat hard for anything in their lives.

"Many of us have thought about sitting down in the White House, but none of us thought we had enough experience. It's one thing to sit down in Mayor Wagner's office or the

U.S. Attorney General's office, but it's another to sit down in the home of the President of the United States."

I said, "From what you've heard about the sit-in in the White House, do you think they did anything that would hurt the sit-in movement?"

"Don't get me wrong. I'm not criticizing the way they sat. From all I can gather, they had the right style and they didn't violate any of the rules. But it's like a Little League ball team deciding to play in Yankee Stadium without asking anybody. We've got plenty of places for them to sit so they can learn their trade. My fear is that a lot of sit-in demonstrators will be discouraged by what they did.

"They'll come home from Washington and their parents will say, 'Did you get to sit in the White House?' If they say they didn't, they'll lose face. Their parents will say, 'Do you mean I spent all that money to send you to Washington so you could sit in the mud in Lafayette Park?' "

"Now that the White House has been sat in and is no longer unconquerable, what is there left for sit-ins to look forward to?"

"I don't really know. There was talk that some of us might go down to the LBJ Ranch and sit in the barbecue pit, but it really isn't the same thing."

INDIANS!

Whenever I get tired writing about politics, I like to write a cowboy script. I've been working on one lately about Lyndon Baines, the famous mayor of Great Bird Falls.

In the opening scene, the tall, kindly mayor is addressing the people in front of the the Great Society Saloon.

"Now, folks," he says, "Ah'm happy to announce that everyone is going to get more water, more schooling, and better medical care, and it is my intention to see that Great Bird Falls becomes the most wonderful town in the country and its citizens the happiest people in the world."

The townspeople cheer, but suddenly a cowboy rides into town, jumps off his horse and says breathlessly, "The Shawnees are fighting with Blackfeet Indians, Mayor!"

"That's no concern of ours," the mayor says.

"But the Blackfeet are being led by Apaches."

"Apaches?" says the mayor incredulously. "How do you know?"

"I have the names of 53 Apaches here in my pocket who are fighting on the side of the Blackfeet."

"Where did you get this list?" the mayor wants to know.

"It was given to me by the Shawnees."

The mayor is grim. "We have no choice but to send in the cavalry to protect the lives of the white women and children."

"But there are no white women and children in the area."

"We'll send some in with the cavalry," the mayor says.

The next scene shows the U.S. Cavalry riding up the canyon into Indian territory. They arrive just as the Blackfeet are about to attack the Shawnees.

The cavalry takes up positions between the two tribes and the colonel announces he has come to protect the lives and property of the white man.

The Blackfeet, furious at the interference, start sending up smoke signals denouncing the U.S. Cavalry and the mayor of Great Bird Falls.

The colonel demands that the Blackfeet surrender and give up their Apaches. The chief of the Blackfeet denies he has any Apaches in his tribe.

"We anti-Apache," he tells the colonel. "All Blackfeet want is freedom."

The colonel goes to see the chief of the Shawnees and asks him to give up, but the chief says the Shawnees are the only ones who can keep the territory from going Apache. He demands the right to clean out the Blackfeet once and for all.

The colonel sends back word to the mayor: "Can't tell the good Indians from the bad Indians. Please send instructions."

The mayor dispatches four deputies who meet with the chiefs and ask them to form a coalition tribe made up of Shawnees and Blackfeet.

Both chiefs say, "Ugh."

In the meantime the Blackfeet and Shawnees start taking pot-shots at the cavalry. So the cavalry starts firing back.

The mayor finally calls on the Organization of Indian Chiefs to help him out.

The grizzled chief of the Organization says to the mayor, "How!"

And the mayor replies, "That's what the hell Ah'm trying to figure out."

"WE SHALL OVERCOME"

There seems to be as much division amongst the people who
want us to get out of Vietnam as there is amongst the people
who want us to stay there.

One day last fall, the Students For a Safe and Sane Dien-
bienphu got into a terrific argument with the Mothers For a
Neutralized Mekong Delta. The two groups were walking
along together in front of the White House when one of the
mothers said she thought we should remain in Vietnam until
the United States had some guarantees from the Ho Chi
Minh regime. This so infuriated one of the students that he
threatened to hit her with a Viet Cong flag he was carrying.

A teacher from the Professors Against Using Tear Gas
Against Buddhist Priests tried to settle the dispute, but he in
turn was accused of being a warmonger by the Coeds For
Militant Peace in Pleiku.

Before any blows were struck, a leader of the Coordinating
Committee to Sink the U.S. Seventh Fleet shouted, "Down
with the bombing of North Vietnam."

"What about South Vietnam?" someone from the Blood
Donors of Hanoi and Haiphong group retorted.

"Down with the bombing of South Vietnam too."

"Pull out of Saigon," said someone from the Citizens For
Free Speech in Hue.

"But first, negotiate," a voice from the Fathers For Peace
and Honor in Tan Phung Phu Organization retorted.

Several pickets turned on him. "Pull out first, and then negotiate," cried a leader of the Soldiers and Sailors Against the
Fourth of July.

"Peaceful negotiations first," retorted one of the Women
For a White Christmas.

"How can we have peaceful negotiations if we don't pull
out?" charged the president of the Society For the Abolish-
ment of Basic Training.

"How can we be sure of peaceful negotiations if we do
pull out?" argued a Moderate Student For a Weak Southeast
Asia Policy.

"Why didn't Rusk agree to negotiate in 1964?" demanded

a man from the Nonviolent Agitation Committee Against World War III.

"Because Hanoi said they never made the offer," screamed a woman with the Daughters Against the Rhodesian Revolution.

"Johnson is lying to us," said a student lighting his cigarette on his draft card.

He offered his draft card to two other students to light their cigarettes.

"Three on a draft card is unlucky," said a startled girl representing Teen-Agers For Total Disarmament.

"The Commies are the liars," heckled a Georgetown U. law major from the Committee to Fly the American Flag Twenty-Four Hours a Day.

"All right, keep moving, keep moving," a policeman from the Benevolent Society For Stronger Law Enforcement said.

"Down with the Army-Navy game."

"Send McNamara back to Ford."

"Bundy is a Buddhist."

And so it went all morning long.

I was just about to take my leave when one of the pickets said, "Who are you with?"

I thought fast. "I'm with the Society of Nonviolent Newspapermen to Permit Luci Johnson to Marry the Man She Loves."

He asked me to join him in singing "We Shall Overcome."

THE GREAT UNWASHED

The real objection to student demonstrations in the United States, as far as I can discover, is not the politics of the students or what they're demonstrating against, but the fact that many of the demonstrators are unwashed and uncombed.

One day Representative Dowdy, of Texas, told the Daughters of the American Revolution at their 74th convention that their arrival in Washington was "a breath of fresh air" compared to the "rabble-rousers, beatniks and bums who so recently have been descending on us."

Many people have been echoing Congressman Dowdy's words. "If they'd only take a bath," a friend told me, "I wouldn't care what they did."

Another man said, "I think if they really believed in America they'd shave." A lady who witnessed the White House Easter demonstrations said, "I don't think those girls shampooed their hair in a year."

And so it goes. There is nothing that disturbs a white-collar worker more than somebody else with a dirty white collar. It is therefore my belief that if we could clean up our demonstrators there would be no objection to their demonstrating. For one thing, you know anybody who looks clean isn't going to be a Communist.

For another, since cleanliness is so close to godliness, you know that a clean demonstrator believes in God, and that's all we ask of our students these days.

I talked to several of the students picketing the White House on the Easter weekend and they agreed with me that cleanliness was quite a problem when you're demonstrating.

"You ride all night on a bus," one student said, "so you're not going to wear your best clothes. Then you have to think in terms of sit-ins. You never know when you're going to be ordered to sit down. Most sidewalks are pretty dirty, you know."

Another student agreed and also said, "You know, demonstrating is hard work and you work up quite a lot of perspiration carrying those signs over your head. Even if you did take a bath it wouldn't help."

A college coed in blue jeans said, "There's no sense putting up your hair because it gets all messed up if you get arrested."

"It isn't as if we're going to a prom," another coed added.

"But there are some pickets who look very neat," I said.

"Oh, those are FBI informers. They have to look neat or they'll ruin their image."

"Besides," the other coed added, "they're the only ones allowed to use the White House washroom."

"Then you're not against baths in principle?"

"Oh, no," a student said. "If they'd let me in the White House I'd take one right now."

"Me, too," another student said. "They must have more than one bath in there."

Only one student said he wouldn't take a bath in the White House. "At least not until they stop bombing North Vietnam."

GREEN PEOPLE ARE COMING

When the flying saucers were sighted over Ann Arbor, Mich., a few weeks ago, the first reaction from one of the residents was, "Dammit, there goes the neighborhood."

It has been reliably reported that occupants of all flying saucers are little green men, and this raises a serious problem. Do we want our children to go to school with little green children? What happens to real estate values when the little green people start moving in on the block? Will the green people be responsible for a rise in the crime rate? These questions have to be answered before there is a mass invasion of them and we have a situation that will make Watts look like a tea party.

I spoke to the president of the NAAGP (the National Association for the Advancement of Green People) the other day.

He said, "We are very concerned about the treatment that the little green people will get when they arrive in the United States. I'm sure that the first few will be cordially received, but as more and more flying saucers arrive, we will have a serious social problem."

"But the Jolly Green Giant has been well received in America," I said.

"Yes, but he's in show business. What we're concerned with is the average green person who has no special skills and is more or less a drag on society."

"What do you think will be the main problem?"

"For one thing, the green people will not be able to read or write English—at least, we don't think they will. So we'll have to make allowances for that. For another, it will be very hard for them to get jobs. Oh, they could probably get work as maids or cooks or waiters, but when it comes to competing for a white-collar job, I don't believe a green person is going to get it."

"Why is that?"

"Most people are nervous about green people. They feel superior to them and at the same time they're afraid of them. It might have something to do with sex."

"What does the NAAGP plan to do about it?"

"We'll go through the courts first. If that doesn't work, we'll have mass demonstrations. The green people have to have the same rights as other people—not only because they're green, but because they're so small."

I spoke to a member of a White Citizens Council who was absolutely opposed to giving green people any rights.

"We're just getting used to black people. We're not going to have green people forced down our throats," he said. "We have a right to choose whom we want to associate with, whom we want to eat with, and whom we want our kids to go to school with. Everyone knows that green people are inferior."

"But the Jolly Green Giant is not inferior."

"I'd like to ask you one question, mister. Would you want your sister . . . ?"

"Please, don't say it."

"I thought so. You left-wing liberals are all alike."

V. TOO HOT IN THE KITCHEN

KENNEDY—MESTA OR FIGHT

As everyone knows, the most important crisis in Washington last summer was when Perle Mesta and Senator Teddy Kennedy both gave parties on the same night in their respective homes.

As times goes on, the bits and pieces of what took place on that fateful night are being put in place and I've been able to put most of them together.

This apparently is what happened:

At three o'clock on Thursday morning all the society editors in Washington were telephoned and told to stand by for an important story.

They weren't given any hint of what it was except that the Joint Chiefs of Staff were holding an emergency session and all caterers in Washington had been put on a red alert.

The society gals immediately started calling their sources and by seven o'clock in the morning it was known that Perle Mesta and Teddy Kennedy were highball to highball and neither one would clink.

What had happened was that Teddy Kennedy had sent out invitations for a dance in honor of his brother Bobby at the same moment that Mrs. Mesta had decided to give a dinner dance for Senator Mike Mansfield.

There is a fail-safe box to prevent this type of accident in Washington, but somehow it didn't work and the invitations were in the air before they could be recalled.

The news hit the town like a thunderbolt. The florists called up their reserves, all leaves of musicians were canceled, dance-floor waxers were brought in from outer bases and hairdressers were put on 24-hour duty.

The President, who happened to be in Texas at the time, was immediately informed of the crisis and held a meeting at his ranch. Some of the staff wanted him to return to Washington immediately to give Mrs. Mesta much-needed support, but other advisers felt it would be best for him to stay in Texas, where he wouldn't have to show his hand.

Mrs. Mesta made a statement on Friday morning saying she wasn't declaring war on the Kennedys and that her party for Senator Mansfield was only a training exercise.

The Kennedys, who remembered that Mrs. Mesta supported Richard Nixon in 1960, scoffed at the denial and redoubled their champagne order. They said they would go ahead with the dance with or without Mike Mansfield.

The society editors, who hadn't had a thing to write about in six months, rushed to their typewriters and began filing thousands of words on the confrontation.

The town started choosing up sides and the cry heard along Pennsylvania Avenue was "Kennedy—Mesta or fight!"

As the time for the parties drew near, the photographers took up their positions in front of both houses, the caterers started moving in their heavy pots and pans, and tough combat-ready bartenders set up their bottles of bourbon and scotch.

The President kept in touch by telephone.

Since the Mesta party was at nine and the Kennedy dance scheduled for eleven, the first champagne bottle to pop was at the Mesta stronghold.

It was the shot heard round the world.

As the evening wore on, guests nervously looked at their watches. When eleven o'clock struck, everyone held his breath.

But as luck would have it, Senator Mansfield lost his nerve. He thanked Mrs. Mesta for the party and then picked up his wife and drove over to the Kennedy dance.

A tragic social holocaust was avoided and President Johnson was advised it was safe to return to Washington.

THE HAWKS, THE DOVES, THE FROGS

A whole new set of terms are now in order concerning the positions people took in Washington last summer. During the

Cuban crisis the town was divided between the Doves and the Hawks and this made life very simple for everybody.

But as our foreign position became more complex so did the designations of people who were involved.

For example, an ultraconservative Hawk is someone who wanted to bomb Hanoi and Peking with atomic weapons.

A moderate Hawk is someone who wanted to bomb Hanoi with conventional weapons and Peking with the hydrogen bomb.

A liberal Hawk is someone who wanted to bomb only North Vietnam, including Hanoi, but reserved the right to pursue Communist planes into China if it became necessary.

An ultraconservative Dove, on the other hand, believed we should bomb all of North Vietnam except Hanoi, and increase our ground commitment to show the North Vietnamese we meant business.

A moderate Dove believed we should bomb only the Viet Cong in South Vietnam and fight for what we now hold until we can get negotiations.

A liberal Dove is one who didn't think we should get out of Vietnam, but also felt there is no reason to be there in the first place. Then there were the Frogs. The Frog designation came into being when President Johnson told a story about a farmer who was kept awake by frogs croaking in a pond all night long.

The farmer finally drained the pond and found only two frogs.

Therefore, according to the President, any Senator who disagreed with the Administration's Vietnam policy, and said so out loud, was a well-meaning, but badly misinformed Bullfrog.

If we only had had Vietnam to worry about, the labeling would have been easy. But there were many people in Washington who agreed with what the President was doing in Vietnam, but disagreed with what he was doing in the Dominican Republic. There were also many people who agreed with what he was doing in the Dominican Republic, but disagreed with what he was doing in Vietnam.

People who were for a strong American policy in the Dominican Republic were Sharks. And those who believed we should never have sent troops into Santo Domingo were Sardines.

So it wasn't strange to have people in Washington who

were known as Hawk-Sharks, Sardine-Hawks, Shark-Doves and Dove-Frogs.

It was rare to find a Frog-Hawk, at least one who would speak for attribution.

Of course, one of the problems was that not everybody stayed with his label. One day an Administration official may have sounded like a Hawk and the next day like a Dove. The State Department people started off as Sharks in the Dominican Republic, then became Sardines and then tried to be Doves.

The President maintained he was neither Hawk nor Dove, Shark nor Sardine, and certainly not a Frog. He saw himself as just a large benign Eagle, flying around with an olive branch in his mouth and a bomb in each claw, willing to sit down with any bird who was willing to sit down with him.

TOO HOT IN THE KITCHEN

The resignation of White House chef René Verdon caught Washington by surprise. The first inkling of it came when, in a warm exchange of letters, French chef Verdon wrote:

MON CHER PRÉSIDENT,
   Je m'en vais. (I am leaving.)

RENÉ VERDON

The President replied:

DEAR MR. VERDON,
   So long. (Je m'en fous.)

LYNDON B. JOHNSON

Coming so soon after the resignation of McGeorge Bundy, some sources here feel the President wants to realign his executive staff so all cooking will be done by either Secretary Rusk or Secretary of Defense McNamara.

But the problem of finding a new chef for the White House is not an easy one. The President has ordered his kitchen cabinet to search for a replacement and many interviews have been held to find the right person.

One such interview took place a few days after Monsieur Verdon resigned.

"Mr. Dupont, you come highly recommended to us."

"Oui, monsieur. I have worked at Maxim's, the Tour d'Argent, Pavillon, 21 and the *France*."

"Very good. What dishes can you make?"

"Quenelles de brochet, noisettes d'agneau, poulet de Bresse à la crème, paupiettes de veau, soufflé Grand Marnier."

"Yes, we know all that. But how do you feel about okra with black-eyed peas?"

"I am sorry. I never concern myself with politics."

"I'm not speaking about politics. Can you make a dish of okra and black-eyed peas?"

"Pardon?"

"Never mind. What about chicken shortcake, plantation style?"

"I am sorry, my English is not so good. I thought you said chicken shortcake, plantation style?"

"I did. Mr. Dupont, you must understand that we are very simple people here and we like simple dishes. Red snapper, tamale pie, barbecued beef, venison chili and potato turnovers. Surely you know how to cook one or two of these dishes?"

"At Maxim's we very rarely had requests for those."

"Well, let's think of something simple. Could you make a deer sausage casserole?"

"Only if they put bamboo sticks under my fingernails."

"Mr. Dupont, are you an American citizen?"

"Yes. I became one three years ago."

"Then you must ask not what your country can cook for you, but what you can cook for your country."

"I want to serve in any way I can."

"Good. Why don't you start with something easy like pinto beans with salt pork?"

"Would you settle for a steak Diane?"

"Mr. Dupont, the White House will never compromise on its cuisine. We entertain heads of state, kings and princesses, emperors, and someday, God willing, President de Gaulle. Do you know why they like to come here?"

"I have no idea."

"Because we serve the best six-shooter coffee in the world."

"Can I go home now?"

"Yes. But don't call us. We'll call you."

PROTECT OUR MAYORS

The Honorable Representative William Dickinson of Alabama put in the *Congressional Record* his charges of sexual orgies in the march from Selma to Montgomery, Ala. While everyone is concerned about these, the main problem seems to be what's happening in Washington, D.C., when a Southern mayor visits this town.

Last spring another Southern mayor, this time from Arkansas, was bilked in a flimflam game in Washington. As with the mayor of Selma, the victim was out on the town looking for fun and games. Instead his guide left him holding a brown envelope with newspaper clippings in it, in what has become known as the "Murphy" game. ("Put your money in this envelope, mister, so it will be safe.")

Many public-spirited citizens in Washington have become deeply disturbed by what is happening to our Southern mayors when they come to the nation's capital. They've decided something has to be done about it, not only to protect their good names, but also to protect the good name of the city.

The trouble seems to be that when a small-town Southern mayor comes to Washington he doesn't have enough to do at night. He's left more or less to his own devices and, not knowing the ways of a big city, he's bound to get into difficulty.

Therefore, a group of citizens have decided to start a sort of USO for small-town mayors, where they could come in the evening and play ping-pong and get hot dogs and hamburgers and meet nice girls from good homes instead of the type they're bound to run into if they're left on their own.

The UMO (United Mayors Organization), as it would be called, would advise mayors on where they could get good clean rooms, what there was to see in Washington, and how to avoid being cheated by undesirable elements in the city.

"Why do you think mayors are so susceptible to the flimflam game?" I asked a spokesman for the UMO.

He replied, "We have mayors coming in all the time, many from small Southern towns, homesick and far from their families.

"If they had a decent place to go in the evenings, they

wouldn't be tempted by all the debauchery in Washington. We owe it to them to see they have someone to talk to, a friendly ear to listen to their troubles, and a person who can keep them from getting their pockets picked.

"I know that if our club had been going, neither the mayor of Selma nor the mayor from the town in Arkansas would have lost any money when they were here."

"Sir, what is your advice to a small-town mayor coming to Washington for a meeting?"

"First of all, he shouldn't speak to strangers, no matter how accommodating they sound. Secondly, if anyone tries to sell him something like the Washington Monument, he should check with a reliable source to make sure the monument hasn't been sold already.

"Thirdly, if anybody suggests 'entertainment' not of a theatrical nature, the mayor should reject the offer and report it to one of our chaperones at the club."

"Isn't it true that many mayors who are afraid to integrate at home are trying to do it in Washington, D.C.?"

"That seems to be the problem," he said. "We believe in integration, but we don't think it should take place after twelve o'clock at night. That's when all the trouble starts."

HAM ON RYE

It was reported in all the newspapers that the mayor of Bull Whip, Ala., was involved in a flimflam confidence game in Washington, D.C.

There have been so many versions of what happened that I immediately tried to separate the wheat from the grits. This much is certain. The mayor and a friend of his were in Washington, D.C., to appear on a television show called *Closed Mind*. After the show, around one in the morning, they went out into the street, for we know not what, met a friendly Negro, who, when he discovered that the mayor was from Bull Whip, offered to show him the town. In the course of the tour the mayor lost $112, or $5 more than the mayor of Selma, who by coincidence, happened to be out on the town the same evening. It has been established that the mayor of Selma and the mayor of Bull Whip never met during the entire evening.

I called the mayor of Bull Whip for his version. "It's a pack of Northern press lies," he said at once.

"What is, Mayor?"

"Whatever you're going to write."

"Well, sir, I'd be most interested in hearing your version."

"Wal, this is what happened, and may the state police strike me down if I'm lying.

"We finished this here television show about midnight and my friend says to me, 'Let's go out and get us a ham and cheese sandwich for some excitement.'

"I says, 'Fine.' I never been to Washington before, and I always wanted to try a ham and cheese sandwich.

"And there standing on this corner is this nigra. He looks just like my bootblack back home, so I feel I can trust him, and I says, 'Boy, you know where we can get us a luscious ham and cheese sandwich, something like we couldn't get in Bull Whip?'

"And this darky grins and says, 'Sure, boss, I can fix you up with a ham and cheese sandwich. I got me a friend that makes 'em real good.'

" 'How much are they?' I asks him.

" 'Well, boss, this is kind of a club and it's $6 membership, $50 each for the sandwich.'

"My friend says, 'Isn't that a little bit expensive for a sandwich?' And the nigra says, 'Food's a big item in this town.'

"Wal, we start haggling with the fellow, 'cause we don't want to be taken for country bumpkins, and I tell him I know what ham costs in Bull Whip and I know what cheese costs and I know what bread costs and it sure couldn't come to $50 a sandwich.

"The nigra says, 'You the guys that says you was hungry.' So I finally say, 'Okay, but I want to look at this ham and cheese sandwich first.'

"The nigra takes us to a strange part of Washington and says, 'You better put your money into this here envelope because you never know what's going to happen in these after-hours restaurants.' So we put the money in an envelope and he disappears. When he don't come back, my friend and I get suspicious and we open the envelope and our $112 is gone.

"It suddenly dawned on us that we're victims of another Yankee crime wave.

"So my friend and I go back to the hotel and we decide everything George Wallace says about Washington, D.C., is true. You give nigras the vote and the next thing you know they're lying and cheating and stealing your money."

"There's only one other question I'd like to ask you, Mayor," I said. "Why didn't you report the incident to the police?"

"Very simple. Who would believe that two men from Bull Whip, Ala., were out at one o'clock in the morning looking for a ham and Swiss cheese sandwich?"

A GREAT MONUMENT

Every once in a while I feel I should come to the defense of Congress. Our Representatives, who are constantly saving us money, looking after our interests and keeping the peace, have been under fire because of a silly building in Washington which has been built to house their new offices.

The Rayburn House Office Building was built to take care of 169 Congressmen and their staffs. It is modest in proportions and takes up only two city blocks. The architects, builders and Congressmen managed to complete the entire thing for only $125 million, which in these days of high prices for marble and carpeting is a bargain.

Originally the building was supposed to cost only $64 million, but unfortunately this price didn't include the plumbing and welcome mats, and although the estimate was more than doubled, I see no reason why the American taxpayers should complain.

Architecturally, the building has been a great success and has been compared with some of the finest state penitentiaries in the country.

It has been called "Edifice Rex," "Forest Lawn East" and "The Seventh Blunder of the World" by some critics who don't know a good thing when they see it.

But the majority of people are happy with its simple lines and modest grandeur.

"Only Mussolini could have built something like this," an architect told me when he saw it.

While it is beautiful from the outside, it is also functional from the inside. For example, although the building is only four stories high, 15 percent of the building has been allocated for offices and hearing rooms, and the rest of the space has been set aside for hallways, staircases and parking space for 1,100 automobiles.

Eight of the nine rooms set aside for permanent committees are two stories high and seat as many as 130 people. There hasn't been one wasted inch of room in the entire building.

Each Congressman has his own washroom and safe, but his suite of offices has been designed in such a way that if he wants to speak to his aide or staff he has to walk through his waiting room.

This gives the Congressman ready access to his constituents, which is the way the architects planned it.

There are: a 60-by-20-foot swimming pool, a 112-by-40-foot gym, five dining rooms, a cafeteria and a courtyard.

The art work has also been praised by many. One critic called it the greatest example of Bolshevik modern in this country.

Another said that students would come from all over the world to stare at the art work in amazement.

In any case, the criticism of the Rayburn House Building has been unjustified. You can't build a $125 million office building without making mistakes, and if there was any hint that the building was a waste of taxpayers' money, Congress would certainly investigate it. Wouldn't they?

"FUN" FOR THE SNOWDONS

As everyone had been reading, Washington was gaga over the November 15th arrival in town of Princess Margaret and Lord Snowdon. The excitement had been mounting and it was hard to contain yourself when you realized that the Princess and her husband would be here in less than a week.

The word had gone out that Princess Margaret and Lord Snowdon wanted to have "FUN." They wanted to meet young, gay, and amusing people while they were in the United States because, as one society reporter aptly put it, "they're so young, gay and amusing themselves."

The instructions were so explicit in regard to the type of people the royal couple wanted to meet that hostesses in Washington were hard put to fill the bill.

I received a panicky call from a hostess who said, "You've

got to help me. I can't find any young, gay, and amusing people in Washington."

"Well," I said, "some people would still consider me young, I'm rather gay, and, goodness knows, I'm amusing."

"You don't understand," she said tearfully. "Princess Margaret and Lord Snowdon prefer offbeat people to stuffy ones. I don't know any offbeat people."

"Have you tried the Supreme Court?"

"Please be serious," she said. "Oh, why doesn't Washington have a jet set?"

"I guess because they won't let jets land at National Airport."

"Surely," she said, "you must know some characters in town."

"Have you tried the White House?"

"They're having trouble themselves," she said. "Most of the offbeat people they've invited have refused to come as a protest over President Johnson's policy in Vietnam."

"It does present a problem," I admitted.

"I need beautiful people who can dance and talk and who are terribly clever."

"It sounds like a job for the Teamsters Union."

"You're making fun of me," she wailed.

"No, I'm not. I'm very sympathetic to your problem. What about Congress? There must be some gay, amusing, young, offbeat dancers and talkers there?"

"Yes, but they're not mad, mad, mad people."

"Have you tried the Pentagon?" I asked.

"They're beautiful, but they're not amusing. The State Department are amusing, but they're not beautiful. Oh, what am I going to do?"

"If you get in real trouble," I said, "my wife can do a flamenco dance on a bridge table."

She refused to pick up the hint.

"Why don't you look at it this way?" I said. "Everybody is inviting young, gay, amusing, offbeat people to parties for the Snowdons. By the time they get to your house they might welcome meeting some dull, stuffy people, just for a change of pace."

"I never thought of that," she said excitedly. "My party for Princess Margaret would be different and something she would always remember. I'll give the only dull and stuffy party she'll have in the United States."

"What will you put on the invitations?" I asked.

"Come as you are."

DIG WE MUST

Washington just had one of the biggest blizzards in its history and, although snow had been predicted, no one thought it would be on this scale. One of the reasons for this is the credibility gap where people are suspicious of everything that is announced in the nation's capital.

I discussed this with a high government official as he was digging his car out of the driveway Monday morning. "Sir, did you know there was going to be a blizzard Saturday night?"

"I'm as surprised as anybody," he said. "I heard that bad weather was in the works, but I thought this was just a way of President Johnson making it easier to announce he was going to resume the bombing of North Vietnam."

"Who authorized the blizzard?"

"It had to come from the White House. My department certainly knew nothing about it. We weren't even consulted."

"Do you think a blizzard was a good thing to have at this time of the year?"

"Well, you have to remember the President is the only one who can make this agonizing decision. He has all the facts. While a blizzard may look like the worst thing to give the people, it could, in the long run, be the best thing we could do under the circumstances."

"There are some people who believe Congress should have decided whether we should have had a blizzard or not."

"Congress gave President Johnson a vote of confidence in 1965 and said they would support any decisions he made concerning the weather."

"Yessir, but they thought they were voting for a light snowfall or at the most a white Christmas. They had no idea the President was going to get us into a blizzard."

"The President didn't want a blizzard any more than anybody else. For the last three months he has done everything to keep the weather from getting out of hand. But the elements have been against him and it is his opinion that, unless we stand firm in the face of heavy snowfall now, we will have a worse blizzard later on. Everyone in this Administration is for clear weather, but it has to be clear weather with honor."

"Isn't one of the dangers of a blizzard that the harder you try to dig out of it, the more chance you have of getting stuck in it?"

"Nobody knows the dangers of a blizzard more than the President. He did not arrive at his decision to have one until he consulted with many, many people."

"Was Dean Rusk in on it?"

"I'm sure of it. He had to notify our allies what we plan to do."

"Have they supported him in the blizzard policy?"

"They haven't been given snow plows or road-clearing equipment, and there are some of our friends who asked the President to hold off on the blizzard indefinitely and give the elements a chance. But here again the President had to make the final decision."

"Could this lead to larger and larger blizzards?"

"We certainly hope not. The dropping of snow at this time should indicate that we mean business and, although we may be up to our necks in snow, this doesn't mean we wouldn't be the first ones to want it all to melt."

"What happens if the blizzard doesn't work?"

"We'll have to cook up some other kind of storm."

"It looks as if it's going to snow some more," I said.

"I'm sure the President would allow no more snow to drop than is absolutely necessary."

THE PET SHOW

The Northwest Settlement House in Washington, D.C., held a charity pet show at Hickory Hill, the home of Senator and Mrs. Robert Kennedy, and as luck would have it, I happened to be one of the judges.

Judging a pet show can be a very difficult proposition under any circumstances, but judging one at the home of the Kennedys can be almost impossible. It is no secret the Kennedys like to win at anything they compete in, and a pet show is no exception.

When I first arrived, Ethel Kennedy said she didn't want to do anything to influence my judging, but she introduced me to each of her children "just so you will know who they are."

There were about 500 children, including my own, competing for nine classes of prizes, and each mother kept a beady eye on me as I tried to judge the winners.

The first category gave me no trouble because it had to do with cats and the Kennedys had failed to enter it.

But I knew I was in trouble with the second class, which was feathered birds. One of the Kennedy children had entered two birds in this class and, when he only won second prize, a look of horror appeared on Ethel Kennedy's face. I shrugged my shoulders and tried not to look at her.

The next class was fish and the first prize went to the person with the largest fish. Bobby Kennedy, Jr., had gone to his pond and brought back a trout, which put everyone else's goldfish to shame.

I had no choice but to give him a blue ribbon. Many of the mothers started muttering and we were forced to make an announcement: "The judges would appreciate it if Mrs. Kennedy did not applaud so loudly when one of her children wins a prize."

In the trick class, the oldest of the Kennedy children, Joe Kennedy, produced a giant Newfoundland named Brumis. Brumis's tricks consisted of attacking other dogs, children and adults, and Mrs. Rowland Evans, the chairman of the pet show, ordered him out of the ring. Joe Kennedy and Ethel Kennedy were in tears.

Then we got to the most unusual pet class. This was a tough one, because one of the Kennedy children brought in either a large lizard or a small alligator. My eight-year-old daughter had entered a hamster and I was in a tough spot. Mrs. Kennedy kept tugging my arm and my daughter kept tugging my shirt. I decided that there was a tie for first place—the Kennedy child for the most unusual pet and my daughter was given first prize for "the most unusual hamster entered by a child whose father was a judge."

This didn't go over very well with the other mothers, or with the fathers who were there. Teddy Kennedy wanted to know why his kid didn't get a prize for her goldfish and Mrs. Stephen Smith, sister of Teddy, insisted her son's snake had been discriminated against. I gave them honorable mentions.

The dog class gave me the most trouble. For one thing, Mrs. Kennedy sent Brumis back into the ring, and he had to be thrown out again. For another, almost every child there had a dog, including my own son's basset hound. I pretended

I didn't know who my son was and gave him a blue ribbon for having the dog with the longest nose, and then I gave Sargent Shriver's daughter a blue ribbon for best pair of dogs in the show. This made Mrs. Donald Wilson, wife of the Deputy Director of the USIA, furious and she threatened to report me to the Westminster Kennel Club. Mrs. Shriver said that if Mrs. Wilson did it, she would put in a good word for me.

The Kennedys, the Shrivers, and the Smith children walked off with about 20 blue ribbons and five Secret Service men had to escort me off the grounds through a crowd of lynch-minded mothers. But it could have been worse. Lyndon Johnson could have entered his beagle, and then I really would have been in a fix.

VI. "OH SAY CAN YOU SEE?"

"OH SAY CAN YOU SEE?"

The cynics may scoff and the left wingers may grumble, but the Daughters of the American Revolution pulled off their biggest coup of 1965 when they got a New York girdle manufacturer to withdraw from the market a red, white and blue garment called "Stars 'n Stripes."

The pop art girdle made by the Treo Company was attacked by the D.A.R.'s flag committee, who called it "a shocking caricature and a desecration of the American flag."

The president of the Treo Company immediately announced he was withdrawing the girdles from distribution and they would either be destroyed or given to a "foreign charity."

It would be a pity if the Treo Company destroyed these girdles, particularly since so much time, effort and imagination went into them.

At the same time I can't help agreeing with the Daughters of the American Revolution that no red-blooded American woman should wrap herself in the Stars and Stripes, which represents, if you'll excuse the expression, the foundation of our liberty.

So I would buy the Treo Company's second idea, which is to send the girdles abroad.

It is a known fact that 70 percent of the people in the world who receive American foreign aid have no idea who gave it to them. The Communists in many countries are constantly removing the U.S. aid stickers on the gifts, and there have been situations where they have even substituted the hammer and sickle.

This would be the first opportunity for us to give some-

thing to a foreign country where there would be no mistaking its point of origin. By giving American Stars 'n Stripes girdles to a needy nation, we would not only gain a great propaganda victory in the cold war, but we would also win the battle for the minds of men.

I believe that in order to have the most impact, the girdles should be distributed in backward nations where they could replace the sarong or the grass skirt as the only garment worn by a native woman. In this way the Stars and Stripes would be on display day and night, reminding everyone that even in the jungle the United States is always there.

One suggestion was made that the girdles be sent to Vietnam so our GIs could tell the loyal Vietnamese women from the Viet Cong women, but there was some fear that they might fall into the hands of the Viet Cong and confuse everybody.

It was also feared that the Stars 'n Stripes could cause friction between American and South Vietnamese troops. So that idea was abandoned.

A third suggestion was to give them to the Soviet Union to show them how far ahead of them we are in the race to contain space.

But the D.A.R. rejected the idea on the grounds that supplying the Soviet Union with girdles would only give aid and comfort to the enemy.

While they've probably got a point, I still believe that we would be losing a great opportunity to do some good abroad if we destroyed the objectionable garments.

The D.A.R. deserves credit for calling the red, white and blue girdles to the attention of the American public, and Treo deserves credit for agreeing to yank them off the market.

Now it's the government's turn to decide what they're going to do about it. An aid official told me: "First we're going to send one up a flagpole to see who salutes."

THE "NEW GERMAN" MOVIE

Word has come in from West Germany that many of the German people are getting tired of being shown as heavies in World War II. They feel it's about time motion picture producers and writers stopped showing the Germans in a bad light and that everyone forgot about their past mistakes.

I couldn't agree with them more. The German people have suffered enough at the hands of Warner Brothers and MGM, and an effort should be made to forget the past and give the Germans a new image.

One of the main problems in the previous war movies is that the Nazis are played by such disagreeable types. They're always snarling and shouting, "Heil Hitler!" and slapping pretty French Resistance girls in the face.

If we really want to do them a service, I think we should pay more attention to casting. In the new war pictures, we should cast Pat Boone, Pat O'Brien or Jimmy Stewart as the SS men, and Otto Preminger, Paul Lukas, and Helmut Dantine as the American GIs.

This would be a start in conjuring up sympathy for the German side. Once you solve the casting problem, you have to think about plot. First, we must get away from the stereotyped German U-boat commander.

I see a picture where Pat Boone is commander of a German U-boat. He is out searching for prey.

His executive officer, played by Lawrence Welk, says, "Sir, I've got a target in the periscope."

Boone grabs the periscope and says, "It's the *Athenia,* a passenger ship."

Welk says, "When should we fire?"

Boone pulls the periscope down. "We can't. There are women and children aboard."

"But they've seen us. They'll radio our position."

"I'd rather risk getting sunk than torpedo a ship with civilians aboard. Hitler would want it that way."

Another image we must change is that of the role of the Gestapo in World War II.

In the *nouvelle-vague* World War II film, we would show Gestapo headquarters in Paris with Bing Crosby playing the head of the Gestapo. They have just brought in Pierre le Loup, head of the entire French Resistance.

Crosby says, "Loup, we want the list of every Resistance fighter in France."

Pierre le Loup says, "You'll never get it out of me."

"We have ways of getting things out of people." Crosby rings a buzzer and Fred MacMurray comes in. Crosby says to Fred MacMurray, "He doesn't seem to be in the mood to talk."

MacMurray replies, "Well, there's nothing we can do about it. If we lay a finger on him we'll have to answer to Himmler for police brutality."

The other standard plot that has been showing the Germans in a bad light has to do with prisoner-of-war camps. A new version, which could be called *Stalag Hilton,* would star Henry Fonda as the camp commandant.

Doris Day would play his wife, who rolls bandages for the Jewish prisoners in the hospital.

Glenn Ford, the SS sergeant, rushes in, shouts, "The prisoners are escaping, Herr Commandant."

"Don't talk to me," Fonda says. "I'm in on the July '44 plot to kill Hitler."

And Ford says, "Aren't we all?"

THE LONELIEST WEEKEND

The last weekend of 1965 was probably the loneliest weekend of the year for American wives and sweethearts. There were eight football games scheduled for those three days and they were all being shown on television, much to the consternation of American husbands who would rather have spent the time with their families and loved ones.

The American man had no choice. He had nothing to do with the television football schedule or the escalation of the various bowl games by the networks.

"I don't like it any more than my wife," my friend Ben said, "but the sponsors are putting up a lot of money to telecast these games and I owe it to them to watch as much football as I can."

His wife was philosophical about it. "I'd be lying if I said I wasn't going to miss Ben for the next three days, but I'll have the children and they will be a great comfort to me."

My friend Phil's wife seemed to take it harder. She was crying when I called. "Every year it's the same thing. He goes into the library on Friday afternoon for the East-West Shriners game and I don't see him until the NFL pro championship game is over on Sunday."

"It's a lie," Phil said on the extension phone. "I always come out at midnight to wish her a happy New Year."

"Yes," she sobbed, "but your eyeballs are so glassy you can't even see me."

"Leave my eyeballs out of this," Phil shouted.

I called a third friend, Larry, who said, "I think the women have a point. The New Year's weekend is no fun for them anymore. So I've given it up."

"Given what up?" I asked him.

"I've given up the Gator Bowl game on Friday afternoon. I'll only watch seven games this year."

"You've got a lot of heart, Larry," I said.

"Well," he replied, "a man's marriage has to come first."

I called up Bill, a friend of mine, and asked him if his wife was giving him any trouble about the weekend.

"Hell, no," he said, "she just packed up and left."

"Left? Where did she go?"

"I don't know. She said something about Reno and getting a divorce."

"Aren't you upset?"

"Why should I be? She has no grounds. I've got the grounds for a divorce. Do you know what she did? She invited her mother and father to come over on New Year's Day. How do you like that? She knew about the Sugar Bowl, the Cotton Bowl, the Rose Bowl, and the Orange Bowl, and she still invited them over. There isn't a judge in the country who wouldn't be outraged by what she did."

"It's a case of mental cruelty if I ever heard one," I said.

"Do you know what else she did?"

"I hate to ask."

"She tried to break the television set before she left."

"But that's a crime of passion," I said.

"My lawyer says she's lucky if she doesn't get ten years."

A final telephone call illustrated what great turmoil this country was in. I called my friend Carey and asked him how his wife felt about the long weekend.

He said sadly, "She's going to watch all the games with me. She said it's the wife's duty to stay at her husband's side, no matter how rough the going gets. She also says all the kids are going to watch the games, too."

"What are you going to do?"

"What am I going to do? I'm going out to the movies by myself and see *Thunderball*."

THE BRIDGE CHEATERS

As everyone knows by now, the biggest story of the year was the bridge-cheating scandal at the 13th annual World Contract Bridge Team Tournament in Buenos Aires. Two British players, Terence Reese and Boris Schapiro, were accused of using signals to tell each other how many hearts they were holding. They were said to use finger movements, and the evidence was damaging enough for the non-playing British captain to default his team's points.

The impact of this revelation has made a tremendous impression on the bridge world, not only with professionals but amateurs as well. The other evening I was over at a friend's house where four people who had been playing bridge for years started a game.

After the first hand was dealt, one friend, whom I'll call George, said to one of the opposing players, Fred, "Why did you do that?"

"Do what?" Fred wanted to know.

"Scratch your head."

"Because it itched," Fred said heatedly. "What do want me to do with my head when it itches?"

"Why didn't you scratch your head before I dealt?"

"Because it didn't itch before you dealt. What are you trying to say, anyway?"

"Never mind. It just seems strange that I never saw you scratch your head before."

"Well, it so happens I scratch my head a lot. Do you want me to tell you before I'm going to scratch my head?"

"Why can't you scratch your head after the bidding?"

"I will if it itches after the bidding. But what's the sense of scratching it if it doesn't itch?"

"Come on," Hilda said. "Will somebody bid?"

A few hands later I asked if any one wanted anything to drink. Everyone said, "Yes," and I served them.

George picked up his glass in one hand and held his cards in the other. He said, "Two hearts."

Fred said, "Why did you pick up your glass with four fingers on the outside?"

"How else are you supposed to pick up a glass?"

"I use three fingers."

"You use three, I use four," George said angrily.

"It's strange that you would pick up your glass with four fingers and say, 'Two hearts.' "

"What the hell's so strange about it?"

"People usually don't take a drink while they're bidding."

"I was thirsty."

"I'm thirsty, too, but I never lift my glass until the bidding's over."

"Are you accusing me of something, Fred?"

"I don't know. But I'll be interested to see how many hearts you have."

"Well, if you're so interested, why don't you bid?"

"I bid three spades."

"You scratched your head again. I saw it!" George shouted.

"It itched again."

"How come it only itches when you bid spades?"

"It doesn't only itch when I have spades. The last time it itched I bid diamonds."

"Then you admit you're signaling to your partner," George screamed.

"I admit no such thing. And I refuse to play with a cur like you," Fred said, throwing down his hand.

"That goes double for me," George replied. "Any man that uses four fingers to lift his glass and then bids two hearts has to be cheating."

The two couples walked out of the house and haven't talked to each other since. It looks as if bridge will never be the same again.

FRONTIER PEDDLER

I read a book called *Only You, Dick Daring,* by Merle Miller, which was an exposé of the television business, and the problems of getting a television pilot made. I thought it was an exaggeration until I got an idea for a television show myself and tried to get somebody interested.

My idea was to do a show called *Frontier Peddler* which was to be a series based on the peddlers who traveled through the West selling their wares on horseback. My hero, whom I wanted played by Edward G. Robinson, would have one thing going for him. Although his clothes were grotesque and he looked like a poor peddler, he was, in fact, a very fast man with a gun—he had to be to stay alive. But he had no reputation as a fast gun because no one wanted to admit he could be taken by a peddler.

In the meantime, he goes through the series doing good to everybody, saving people's homes, making chicken soup for sick children, shooting badmen, and bringing joy and philosophy to the world.

As soon as I developed the idea, I immediately took it to my agent, who got terribly enthused. "It's great. I can see Dick Van Dyke playing the peddler."

"I was thinking more of Edward G. Robinson."

"Edward G. Robinson? You must be crazy. You have to have a young peddler, someone the audience can identify with."

"Yeah, I guess you're right," I said.

"I'll set up an appointment with one of the major studios."

Two days later we met with the head of one of the studios.

He loved the whole thing. "It's great and it's different. But why don't we have two young peddlers instead of one, and they're always trying to get each other's girl and each week they have to help someone in trouble. I see it as a Western *Sunset Strip*. In fact, we could have a third kooky fellow who takes care of their horses. It really has a lot of promise. Let's get together with the network people. I'm sure they'll go for it."

We got together with the network people—at least two of them—and I could see I grabbed them from the start. They liked everything about it, except they had one suggestion.

"Why do they have to be peddlers?" one of the executives asked.

"Well," I said, "I figured no one had ever done a series about peddlers before and it would be different."

"People don't care about peddlers. Suppose we kept the idea just as you have it, but instead of a peddler we make the hero a hired gun. We could get somebody like Jim Garner or Chuck Connors. Now this guy sells his services to anyone who needs him, providing, of course, they're on the side of good. Every week he rides into another town and has a problem which he resolves before the show is over."

The other network executive said, "Hey, that's great. The

guy's not married so he can get involved with a girl in each sequence."

"But what about the peddler clothes?" I asked.

"What do you mean, peddler clothes? The guy wears an all-black cowboy suit. That's his trademark."

After we left the meeting, I said to my agent that I didn't think too much of the idea.

"Fortunately," he said, "we have two other networks, so if you don't like the idea we just go to another network."

We went to another network and explained the idea. They loved it but they had only one minor change.

"Instead of two young peddlers, why don't we make them 'Frontier Lawyers' and have a father and son team who go around defending innocent people? I sort of see E. G. Marshall as the father."

At that moment I decided to give up the television business and stick with the column.

IN GM'S DEFENSE

As one who is always looking for lost causes, I think it's about time somebody came to the defense of General Motors. This poor struggling company is being picked on, and harassed, by a Senate Investigating Committee. Why? Because GM had innocently hired a detective agency to look into the private life of a Senate witness who had written a book attacking the safety of one line of its cars.

Not only has this caused the company sorrow and anguish, but it is a direct threat to our free enterprise system.

If an organization, with nothing but the highest motives, can be criticized for inquiring into the sex life and private habits of an individual who wrote a book about it, then we are much farther on the road to a police state than anyone thinks.

Let us look at all the facts. A Mr. Ralph Nader wrote a book titled *Unsafe At Any Speed,* which pointed up the safety hazards in modern automobiles because of structural defects.

This was a very un-American thing to do because, as a former Secretary of Defense once said, "What's good for General Motors is good for the country." Therefore, when Mr.

Nader attacked General Motors he was attacking the country.

General Motors had no choice but to find out what kind of man Mr. Nader was. The only way they could do that was to hire a reputable private detective agency.

This agency was instructed to look into Mr. Nader's sex habits on the valid theory that anyone who doesn't like General Motors' products must be weird.

They couldn't find anything bad about Mr. Nader's sex life, which only shows you what a sneaky guy he is.

When they struck out in *that* department, the detectives did the only honorable thing. They had him tailed.

Senator Robert Kennedy, as well as others on the committee, was incensed about this, but how can you have a healthy and growing economy if you don't follow people around?

The problems raised in this particular situation go much deeper than whether our cars are safe or not. We must be concerned with protecting all corporations who are attacked by individuals. We can't allow people like Mr. Nader to invade the privacy of General Motors.

The Senate Subcommittee hearings have proved, if nothing else, that laws are needed to protect our large corporations.

For a start there should be a law that anyone who writes a book about a company must reveal his sex habits on the back cover.

Legislation must be passed to keep witnesses from testifying against automobile manufacturers.

Presidents of corporations must be spared the embarrassment of having to publicly apologize for doing what is a commonly accepted practice in industry.

The saddest sight I think I'll ever see is when the General Motors president, James M. Roche, had to sit in front of a Senate Committee, with his counsel Ted Sorensen at his side, and read a statement asking Mr. Nader's forgiveness for what General Motors had done to him.

It was a heartbreaking moment for all of us who believe in the underdog, and who feel GM got the raw end of the deal.

LIZ AND I

I read with interest the autobiography of Elizabeth Taylor in the *Ladies Home Journal*. But I was disappointed no end to note that she had not mentioned the important role I played in her life.

The first time I met Elizabeth Taylor was when we were both street urchins in London. I remember her saying to me, "Arthur, when we grow up, will you marry me?"

I patted her on the shoulder and said, "Elizabeth, my family wants me to go to Sandhurst and then on to Oxford. You'd only be in my way."

The years passed, and one day I was driving down a street in Paris when I saw this lovely flower girl. I stopped the car and told the chauffeur to wait. I said to her, "Your face looks familiar."

"It should, Arthur," she said, smiling. "I'm little Elizabeth Taylor who used to play with you in the streets of London."

"So you are," I said. "How much are you selling the flowers for?"

"One franc for the bunch."

"I'll give you a half franc. They seem quite wilted."

"Thank you, Arthur. You were always a kind person."

"Keep well, Elizabeth," I warned. "It's quite damp this time of year." And then I got into my car and drove off. The flowers died in a couple of days.

As you all know, I joined the Royal Air Force and shot down 65 German planes. But in the last hunt I was wounded. They brought me to a hospital in Sussex. One day I saw this Red Cross girl distributing cigarettes to the patients.

"Could your name be Elizabeth?" I asked.

"Yes, Arthur, it's me. I joined the Red Cross to forget."

"Forget what?"

"You," she said, as tears welled up in her eyes.

Tears started to well up in mine. "You know I have a bad leg," I said.

"It doesn't matter, Arthur," she said, sobbing.

"Well, it should," I said. "I think I ought to get two cartons of cigarettes instead of one."

After the war was over, I went into the banking business with my father, and one day I had to fly out to California. While there, I decided to go for a swim in the Pacific above Malibu. But I got a cramp in my bad leg. I shouted for help, and suddenly, swimming out to me, I saw Elizabeth.

"Hold on, Arthur, I'm coming." She brought me in to shore.

"Thank you, Elizabeth. I swallowed a little water, but I don't imagine that was your fault."

"I don't know what I would have done," she said, "if you had drowned."

"It would have been hard to explain to the authorities," I admitted. "Tell me, what are you doing now?"

"I'm a movie actress, Arthur."

"Is that so? I imagine you make quite a bit of money."

"A million dollars a picture. But money doesn't mean anything to me, Arthur."

"It should, Elizabeth. Why don't you open an account with my bank? We pay four percent and there are no charges for writing checks."

I went back to London the next week and forgot all about Elizabeth until one day when I happened to be strolling down the Via Veneto in Rome. There was Elizabeth, gorgeous as ever and, as usual, glad to see me.

"I'm making *Cleopatra,*" she said excitedly. "Arthur, have you ever married?"

"No," I said. "There is only one girl I ever wanted to marry."

Elizabeth started weeping. "Who was that?"

"Baby Jane Holzer. But she married somebody else."

Then Elizabeth said a funny thing. She said, "I'm going to marry Richard Burton, Arthur."

"Why him?"

"Because I couldn't wait for you any longer, Arthur. Don't you understand?"

"Yeh, I guess so. Well, lots of happiness. And if you want to open a joint bank account, let me know."

That was the last time I saw Elizabeth Taylor. But occasionally I hear that people say, even to this day, when they see her, "Isn't that the girl who had the unhappy love affair with Art Buchwald?"

WIN ONE FOR HOFFA

Mr. James R. Hoffa, of the Teamsters Union, has offered to organize all the professional athletes in the United States into his union. The sport that needs it the most, they say, is pro football. While there may be many advantages to having the pro football players in the Teamsters Union, there could be some disadvantages, as you will see if you come into the locker room of the Washington Toughskins. It is half time and the Toughskins are behind 34 to 0.

The coach is standing in front of his blackboard.

"You're playing like a bunch of bums. Higgledorf, why didn't you take out the left end on play number 31?"

"I'm not supposed to take out ends. The union contract says I only have to take out tackles. If I took out the end, I'd be taking a job away from a blocking back."

The coach, trying to keep his temper: "All right, let's forget that. Mickazinski, why did you drop that pass that was right in your arms?"

"I caught my quota for the half. If I caught another one, the guys would have thought I was trying to speed up the game."

"Well, if you drop another pass, I'm pulling you out of the game and putting Wallnicki in."

"You can't do it. I've got three years' seniority over Wallnicki. If you pull me out, the entire team walks off the field."

The coach clenches his teeth. "Harrison, you're the foreman as well as the quarterback. Can't you get any more work out of the men?"

Harrison says, "You're lucky we're here at all. We're not supposed to play on Sunday."

The coach says, "But you're getting time-and-a-half."

"We want double pay, and we also want to be paid for the time we spend going to and from the locker room."

"All right, bring it up at contract time. But right now I'm concerned with winning the game. The defense has been lousy. What happened to you, Brantowski, when they made that hole through off center?"

"I was resting. It says here, 'The linebackers are entitled to take a rest after every three plays.' If I didn't take the rest, I would have been fined by the union."

The coach wheels on his defensive back.

"And where were you, Eberhardt, when they threw the screen pass?"

"Screen passes aren't in my jurisdiction. My job is to cover the flanker. If you want me to cover screen passes, you're going to have to get authorization from the local."

"Okay, okay," the coach says. "Now I wasn't going to tell you this, but it looks as if I've got to. Just before Jimmy Hoffa went to the Supreme Court to appeal his jail sentence, he said to me, 'Coach, if ever things get rough, and the team is down, and they're getting the hell beat out of them, tell them—tell them to win one for The Hoffa.' "

Tears start welling in the players' eyes.

"Gee, coach," the halfback sobs, "you wouldn't be kidding us?"

The coach looks at them. "Those were the last words Jimmy Hoffa said to me. Well, what do you say, team?"

The foreman jams on his helmet and shouts, "LET'S GO OUT THERE, GUYS, AND MURDER THE BUMS."

TAKE AN ARTIST TO LUNCH

One Monday last June was Culture Day at the White House and it certainly was an impressive sight to see. There was sculpture on the lawn, paintings in the hall, singing in the East Room, dancing in the Rose Garden, and, except for McGeorge Bundy's daily briefing to the President, everyone had a wonderful time.

Nobody is quite sure how the White House Festival of the Arts came about, and now that it's over I can reveal the background.

One evening last winter President Johnson was reading a book. Suddenly he turned to Mrs. Johnson and said, "Say, this fellow Robert Lowell writes some mighty pretty poetry. We ought to have him over to the house for lunch."

Mrs. Johnson replied. "What a wonderful idea. Who should we invite with him?"

"How about that fellow Saul Bellow who wrote that best seller, *Her*, about my dog."

"*Herzog*, Lyndon, and it wasn't about your dog."

"Well, it reminded me of my dog."

"Why don't we have John Hersey?" Mrs. Johnson said.

"Did he write *For Whom the Bell Tolls?*"

"No, Lyndon, he wrote *A Bell for Adano*."

"Yeah, let's have him."

"We can't just have writers," Mrs. Johnson said. "Why don't we have some musicians?"

"Lady Bird, are you escalating on me again?"

"No, I'm not. But it would be sort of fun if we asked people from the other arts."

"You make up the list, Lady Bird, and I'll think of a nice toast after lunch."

A month later the President said, "You ever heard from Robert Lowell about lunch?"

"Not yet," Lady Bird said, "but I've invited the Louisville Symphony Orchestra, Marian Anderson, Helen Hayes, the cast of *The Glass Menagerie*, Duke Ellington, Gene Kelly, and Charlton Heston."

"Gee, I'm not going to get much chance to talk to Robert Lowell, am I?"

"Now, Lyndon, you have to be nice to all the creative people. You can't just single out one poet."

"I guess you are right. I am the President of all artists."

"Speaking of artists, I've arranged to have not only the artists come, but they're going to send their pictures on ahead. I've made an art gallery out of the ground floor of the White House."

"Lady Bird, I wish you'd stick to planting rose bushes on Pennsylvania Avenue."

"Now, hush, Lyndon, and tell me where you want to put the sculpture."

"What sculpture?"

"We've got to show sculpture if we're going to show art."

"This lunch is getting out of hand. I think I'll send Hubert in my place."

"No, you won't. This is our party."

Several weeks before the big event, which had now become known as the White House Festival of the Arts, Mrs. Johnson said:

"Lyndon, I have something to tell you if you promise not to get mad."

"All right, I won't get mad."

"Robert Lowell doesn't want to come to lunch."

"Why not?" the President shouted.

"He doesn't like your foreign policy."

"Well, neither do I! But it's the only one I've got."

THE LAUNDROMAT

There comes a time in every man's vacation when he has to go to the Laundromat. My time came earlier than I had expected and I found myself struggling with not one but two baskets of dirty laundry. I threw one into the machine and then sat down on the bench, watching it as it whirled around.

"What are you in for?" the man sitting next to me asked.

"I got caught playing gin rummy when I was supposed to be watching the kids in the swimming pool," I said. "What did you do?"

"I made the mistake of taking a sunbath next to the house," he replied. "My wife said, 'As long as you're doing nothing why don't you take the clothes to the Laundromat?' I said I wasn't doing *nothing;* I was doing something. I was taking a sunbath. She said, 'That's next to nothing.' So here I am. I never realized there was this much dirty laundry in the world."

"What do you use?"

"I don't know. Just any detergent."

"Don't you use a bleach?"

"I did once, and the towels came out lily white."

"What's wrong with that?"

"They were blue when I put them in. What do you use?"

"I use an all-purpose soap that makes our clothes fluffy and clean because it has no harsh ingredients. Look at my hands. They're so soft you would hardly guess I did any laundry at all."

"My hands are rough all the time. Maybe I'll switch over to your soap. Who told you about it?"

"My mother-in-law."

"I guess she should know."

"Let me ask you something. Do you find it's a mistake to put blue jeans in with sheets?"

"I try to avoid it if I possibly can. But if I only have one basket I don't have a choice."

"Which cycle do you like the best?"

"I like to watch the clothes being rinsed after they've been washed."

"I prefer the drying cycle because then I know I'm almost finished. But sometimes you can get some fun out of the first cycle when the soap starts attacking the clothes. Once two of my sport shirts got all tangled up, and I bet the guy sitting next to me five bucks the blue one would win. But I lost."

"I never thought of betting on laundry."

"I'll tell you one thing. It was more interesting than watching the Sonny Liston–Cassius Clay fight."

"That lady over there has her eye on my Laundromat. I still have another basket to do."

"You better go over and protect it. Women have no mercy in this place."

"How come they look so nice on the beach and so mean when they come here?"

"I've always wondered that myself. Maybe it's because they couldn't get their husbands to come. Hey, look! There's a bra caught in a beach robe."

"Gee, it's as much fun as watching a Sophia Loren movie."

"I'll give you five bucks the beach robe wins," he said.

"You've got yourself a bet," I excitedly replied.

THE CURSE

Most bills are now sent out on perforated business-machine cards that say in large letters DO NOT FOLD, BEND OR MUTILATE. I have a friend who doesn't like to be told what to do with a bill, and one day, to my horror, I saw him fold, bend and mutilate a card right in front of my eyes.

"You shouldn't have done that," I said, quivering. "There is a curse on anyone in the United States who folds, bends, or mutilates a bill."

He laughed at me. "That's an old wives' tale. This is a free country, isn't it?"

"Only if you don't fold, bend, or mutilate."

"You're chicken," he said. "No computer is going to tell me what to do."

I didn't see my friend for several months. Then I finally ran across him in a bar. He was unshaven, dirty and obviously had been on a bender.

"What happened?" I asked.

"The curse," he croaked. "The curse got me."

Then he told me his story. He had sent back the folded, bent and mutilated card to the company and received another card in a week, saying, "We told you not to F. B. or M. This is your last chance."

"I crumpled up the card and sent it back," he said, "still thinking I had the upper hand. Then it started.

"First my telephone went out on me. I could not send or receive any messages. I went down to the phone company and they were very nice until they looked up my name. Then the woman said, 'It says here that you mutilated your bill.'

" 'I didn't mutilate my phone bill.'

" 'It doesn't make any difference what bill you mutilated. Our computer is aware of what you did to another computer and it refuses to handle your account.'

" 'How would your computer know that?'

" 'There is a master computer that informs all other computers of anyone who folds or bends or mutilates a card. I'm afraid there is nothing we can do about it.' "

My friend took another drink. "The same thing happened when my electricity was cut off, and my gas. Everyone was sorry, but they all claimed they were unable to do anything for me.

"Finally payday came, but there was no check for me. I complained to my boss and he just shrugged his shoulders and said, 'It's not up to me. We pay by machine.'

"I was broke, so I wrote out a check on my bank. It came back marked 'Insufficient respect for IBM cards.' "

"You poor guy," I said.

"But that isn't the worst of it. One of the computers got very angry, and instead of canceling my subscription to the *Reader's Digest* it multiplied it. I've been getting 10,000 *Reader's Digests* a month."

"That's a lot of *Digests*," I said.

"My wife left me because she couldn't stand the scandal, and besides, she was afraid of being thrown out of the Book-of-the-Month Club."

He started crying.

"You're in bad shape," I said. "You better go to the hospital."

"I can't," he cried. "They canceled my Blue Cross, too."

RUNNING FOR SHOW BUSINESS

There have been so many show business people going into politics lately that many politicians are considering going into show business.

I spoke to one such politician who said, "I think it's the duty of every citizen, no matter what his profession, to become an actor."

"But what do you know about show business?" I asked him.

"What does Ronald Reagan know about politics?" he replied.

"That doesn't answer the question."

"Look, I can introduce *Death Valley Days* or the *General Electric Theater* as well as Reagan can, if not better. If he is going to take the bread out of my mouth, I'm going to take it out of his."

"But the reason Ronald Reagan is going into politics is not to take the bread out of your mouth. He's personable and people like him and he's always played a good guy. That's all you need to run for office these days. But show business requires talent."

He started to do a little tap dance on his rug. "Who do I remind you of?"

"Senator Dirksen?" I asked.

"No, you fool, Senator George Murphy. I've been watching him on the *Late Show*. There really isn't much to it. It's just a question of image. Now watch this."

He picked up a guitar and played several bars.

"Now who do I remind you of?"

"Strom Thurmond."

"How did you guess?"

"Sir, I don't want to be a spoilsport, but it's much easier for a person in show business to become a politician than it is for a politician to become a show business personality. People pay good money to see someone in the entertainment world, while they get their politicians for free. They expect to be disappointed when they hear a politician, but if you fail in show business the public gets angry."

My friend went over to his couch. He started breathing heavily. "Coach," he said with tears in his eyes, "whenever the chips are down and the team is discouraged, tell them—tell them to win one for the Gipper."

"What are you doing now?"

"Ronald Reagan in *Knute Rockne*. That's the deathbed scene. Now don't tell me he did it any better."

"No, I can't say he did."

He went over to his desk, took out a cream pie from a drawer, and threw it in my face. "Who am I now?"

"Pierre Salinger?"

"Steve Allen, you dope. I saw him do it on a TV show."

"You may have the makings of a show business personality at that," I said, wiping the cream off my suit.

"The trouble with you guys is that you think just because a guy has been a politician all his life he doesn't know anything. We care about things, too."

"I'm not doubting you," I said. "But I want to ask you a question. Suppose you don't make it in show business. Suppose there is nowhere for you to go. What will you do then?"

"I'll probably run for Governor of California."

THE TIGER

The automobile is becoming the No. 1 virility symbol in the United States. Not only are they putting tigers in people's tanks as well as the back seat, but the advertisements keep hinting that you're really not much of a man unless you're driving a Beep Beep or some other fast sports car.

A television commercial showed a sickly-looking fellow who was left out of everything until he bought a certain type of car. Suddenly his entire personality changed, and girls were beating down the windshield to get close to him.

It was a very compelling commercial, and so I decided to try it out. I went down to a Beep Beep dealer and asked him if I could try out the car for the afternoon. If I liked it, I'd buy it. He said okay.

"Where's the safety belt?" I asked.

"When you drive a Beep Beep," the man said, "you live dangerously."

I drove the car out of the garage, and pretty soon my chest started to swell and my muscles started to tremble.

I looked in the mirror and could see a sneer on my face and danger in my eyes.

I put it into second. Suddenly I heard a siren behind me. The cop made me pull over.

"You were doing 30 in a 25-mile zone," he said. "Do you have any explanation?"

"I guess I'm just a tiger," I replied, chortling.

"Well, here you are, tiger," the cop said. "I'll see you down at the jungle."

I took the ticket and drove over to the Georgetown Drug store, which is usually swinging around three o'clock on a

Saturday afternoon, and parked it right in front by the door.

Then I sat and waited until a blonde came out and looked at the car. She came over as I expected; but instead of getting in, she said, "Would you mind moving so I can get my car out?"

I pulled up a little, and she pulled out. I started back when a brunette in a tight knitted suit came over and said, "Have you seen a little boy of six with red hair?"

"No, lady. I'm just here waiting for somebody to break down my windshield."

She walked away in a huff.

I turned up the radio, figuring music never hurt anything, and sure enough, a girl came strutting by with a little French poodle.

The poodle stopped by a white-walled tire and started sniffing.

"He wouldn't," I said to the girl.

"He's been trained to," she replied.

Some of the tiger went out of me.

I started to doubt the commercial when a gorgeous girl in a mink coat came rushing up.

"Are you going somewhere?" she said breathlessly.

"Sure, honey. Where do you want to go?"

Her eyes blazed, and she pointed behind her. "My husband's looking for a parking place." She walked over to her husband and said something to him.

He got out of his car, all six-foot-three of him, and I decided it was time to move on.

"I'm pulling out," I shouted. "Just as your wife asked me to do."

I sped off before he could catch me and took the car back to the dealer.

"Well, how did it go, tiger?" the salesman wanted to know.

I winked at him. "Great, fella, but at this rate I'll die before my time."

THE POP SCULPTOR

One day the Canadian authorities refused to allow 80 wooden crates, which looked like cartons of Brillo soap pads, Kellogg's corn flakes, and Mott's apple juice, to go through customs as works of art. The cartons, painted by American pop artist Andy Warhol, were not, said the Canadians, works of art but merchandise, and subject to $4,000 duty.

I think the Canadians are all wet. A few days after the incident in Canada, I went down to the supermarket to buy some groceries for my wife. On the way home I stopped in at an art gallery where they were holding a pop art exhibit. Unfortunately, the carton of groceries got heavy, and I left them on the floor.

Then, being so moved by what I saw, I left the gallery and went home.

"Where are the groceries?" my wife demanded.

"Oh, my gosh," I cried, "I left them at the art gallery."

"Well, you'd better get them if you want any supper tonight."

I rushed back to the gallery, but I was too late. The groceries had been awarded first prize in the show.

"We've been looking all over for you," the gallery owner said. "Why didn't you sign your work of art?"

"It's not a work of art. It's my dinner for tonight."

The gallery roared with appreciative laughter. "He's not only a great sculptor, but he has humor as well," a judge said.

"You can see that in his work," another judge added. "Notice how the bottle of Heinz catsup is leaning against the can of Campbell's pork and beans."

"I'll never know how he was inspired to put the Ritz crackers on top of the can of Crisco," a lady said to her escort.

"It's pure genius," the escort replied. "Notice the way the Del Monte can of peaches is lying on its side. Even Warhol wouldn't have gone that far."

"I think the thing that really won the prize for him was the manner in which he crushed the Sara Lee cheesecake on the bottom of the box."

"It makes Picasso look sick."

"Look," I said, "I'm very grateful for all these honors, but my wife is waiting for this stuff and I have to get it home."

"Get it home?" the gallery owner said in amazement. "I've just sold it to that couple over there for $1,500."

"The groceries cost me only $18," I replied.

"It isn't the groceries. It's what you did with them. You have managed to put more meaning into a box of Rinso than Rodin put into 'The Thinker.' Nobody will ever be able to

look at a can of Franco-American spaghetti without thinking of you. You have said with this bag of groceries, in one evening, what Rembrandt tried to say in 1,000 paintings."

I blushed modestly and accepted his check. That night I took my wife out to dinner, and the next day I went back to the supermarket and bought another bag of groceries, much more expensive than the previous ones, which I immediately took to the gallery.

But the reviews were lousy. "Success has gone to his head," said Washington's leading art critics. "Where once he was able to produce simple jars of cat food and peanut butter in a wild, reckless, I-don't-give-a-damn-manner, he is now serving up elegant cans of mushrooms and mock turtle soup. The famous touch is gone and all that is left is a hodgepodge of tasteless groceries."

TROUBLE AT THE SUPREME COURT

The Supreme Court got itself into a peck of trouble a few weeks ago when it decided several obscenity cases, some for and some against the prurient interests of the United States.

In one case, the Justices upheld the conviction of Ralph Ginzburg for publishing and advertising pornography; in another, they ruled that *Fanny Hill*, a pornographic novel of the eighteenth century, had some "redeeming social value"; and in a third, they upheld the conviction of a man named Mishkin for selling dirty books.

While the Supreme Court did not resolve any of the problems of obscenity, they fixed it so each piece of pornography would have to be judged on its merits, and this will require a great deal of outside reading.

Let us go to the dining room of the Supreme Court, where the Supreme Court Justices are having lunch.

One of the Justices says to another, "I read *Lashed, Whipped and Abandoned* last night."

"Oh, how was it?"

"It had no literary merit, though I must say it had some redeeming social value at the end. The girl finally joins the Peace Corps."

Another Justice says, "I read *Raped, Warped and Wanton*, which I found patently offensive. It was nothing but a series of erotic scenes, tied together by a man who is trying to stop urban renewal in his neighborhood."

"Do you think it has any value to the community?"

"It depends how you feel about urban renewal."

"I really got stuck with a dog last night," another one of the Justices said. "It was titled *Sinner, Sin Once More.*"

"Did it appeal to your prurient interests?"

"It certainly did. I could hardly put it down."

"Well, we'll have to do something about that book. May I have it next?"

"Somebody else has asked for it. I think you're fourth in line."

"If you let me read it tonight, I'll let you have the one I just finished, *Nude Interlude.*"

"Is it obscene, according to the Roth decision of 1957?"

"It goes far beyond the Roth decision, at least as far as the dominant theme is concerned."

"All right, I'll trade you. I was going to read *Lost in Sodom* tonight, but I found the advertising on the back cover very dull."

"Have you seen the new advertising campaign for *Don Quixote?*"

"No, do you think we've got a case there?"

"I should hope so. Don Quixote is shown attacking a windmill which is in the shape of a bare-breasted woman."

"And what is Sancho Panza doing?"

"He's protecting the windmill. The whole thing has the leer of a sensualist to it. The campaign is a disgrace to the community."

"Who wrote it?"

"Miguel de Cervantes."

"Is he up on appeal?"

"Not yet. But I believe they're going after him in Oklahoma."

"I hope I get to write the decision. I never heard of anything so outrageous."

The clerk of the Court comes in. "A new batch of books has just arrived, gentlemen."

"I get first choice after the Chief Justice," someone cries.

"You had first choice last time," another Justice shouts.

"Can I help it if I'm a fast reader?"

CORN FLAKES AND "THE
FEMININE MYSTIQUE"

Unlike most American husbands, I am very concerned about the problems of the modern American Woman and her struggle for fulfillment. My bible has been *The Feminine Mystique,* and no one admires Betty Friedan, the author, more than I do.

Therefore, the other night when I came home from work and found my wife scrubbing the floor, I said to her, "Do you know who you are?"

"I'm sorry," she said blankly. "What did you say?"

"Do you know who you are? Do you have any identity besides being a wife, a mother and a servant?"

"I don't think so," she replied. "Don't step over there, I just mopped it."

"Aren't you concerned that you've traded in your brains for a broom? Can you stand there and tell me that you are contented, happy and satisfied with your lot?"

"Would you rinse out this pail for me?" she said. "I want to know one thing. Are you trying to start a fight with me, are you trying out a new article idea on me, or are you trying to cover up something that you've done?"

"I'm not doing any of them. But I happen to have read *The Feminine Mystique,* and it occurs to me you should want more out of life than this drab existence that you're leading now."

"I'm baking some homemade bread," she said. "I hope the kids like it."

"Answer my question."

"Well, if you must know, I would really like to be a mailman, but I'm afraid to take the civil-service exam."

"That's right, make fun of me. All over America there are millions of unhappy, unfulfilled women who are searching for a place in the sun, who are nothing but sex objects to their husbands, and you stand there making bread and then tell me you're satisfied."

"I didn't say I was satisfied," she said, "but I figure I've got a pretty good deal and I don't want to louse it up."

"You know why you don't want to louse it up?" I said to

her as she set the table for dinner. "Because you're dominated by me. I've denied you your birthright and destroyed you as an individual."

"Maybe I could join a sit-in at the White House."

"That's not what I'm talking about. By being a mother and a wife you are suffering from a problem that has no name. You are lavishing love and affection on me and the children, and this is causing havoc to your id."

"Now don't start knocking my id," she said, draining the spaghetti into a pan. "I know I look out for you and I take care of the children and I keep the house clean and I entertain well—but nobody's perfect."

She then asked me to make her a drink.

"Ah-hah," I said. "Do you know there are a million known alcoholic housewives in this country and there are another million who are on tranquilizers? Why is that?"

"I have no idea."

"Because they are unfulfilled. They are searching for something they'll never find in their homes."

"Maybe I'll go out and have an affair."

"You don't have to go that far," I told her.

"How far do you want me to go?"

"Outside this house is a whole new world. Go out and embrace it. Find the *real* you."

"I will if you go find the children. Dinner is ready."

Later that night, as she was putting up her hair, I noticed she yawned.

"Why did you yawn?" I asked her.

"I'm tired."

"No you're not, you're suffering from housewives' fatigue," I said triumphantly. "Betty Friedan calls it 'the illness that has no name.' No doctor can get at its cause or cure. You are slowly dying of boredom. Every intelligent, able-bodied woman who has no goal, no ambition to make her stretch and grow, is committing a kind of suicide. Do you think I want to live with that on my conscience the rest of my life?"

"Do you mean to say, everytime I yawn, you feel guilty?"

"Something like that," I admitted.

"Okay, if you want me to take my rightful place in society, I will."

A few nights later I came home from work, and found the front door wide open, the kids in the kitchen eating corn flakes, the dog tearing up the rug and the television set going full blast.

"Where's your mother?" I asked.

"She said to tell you she got a job with Sears, Roebuck and she has to work until nine tonight," my ten-year-old said as she took a swing at her brother.

It took me 20 minutes to get her on the phone. "You come home right away," I shouted. "Do you realize what is going on around here?"

"I'll be home at nine. I've finally found myself. The real me."

"Where?"

"Between the pot-holder counter and ladies' pajamas. Now I know what it is to be fulfilled."

I walked into the kitchen, and my son said, "You want puffed wheat or corn flakes?"

"Corn flakes," I said sadly. "Go easy on the milk."

WHO DISCOVERED COLUMBUS?

While everyone is arguing over who discovered America, there is a controversy now raging amongst the Indian tribes over who discovered Columbus.

The chief of the White Hawks has just issued a statement saying that his ancestors were the first to greet Columbus when he landed, and produced the text of the conversation Columbus had with his uncle of many centuries removed.

"Greetings, White Father," the chief said as Columbus stepped ashore. "What brings you to New Vinland?"

Columbus is said to have looked at his map. "New Vinland? I thought this was the New World."

"It was, White Father, but then Leif the Lucky discovered it."

"Does anyone know about this?"

"Only you and I and some monk mapmakers."

"Can you keep your mouth shut, Indian?"

"What did you call me?"

"Indian. I promised Queen Isabella I'd find a new route to the East Indies. Therefore, you're an Indian."

"And what are you, White Father?"

"I am Columbus, an explorer of Italian birth."

"Wonderful," the chief said. "From now on we'll call today Columbus Day in your honor."

"That's very nice of you, Indian. I hereby take this island and all islands north, south, east, and west of it, in the name of the Queen of Spain."

The chief looked at Columbus. "Are you some kind of a nut?"

"What do you mean by that, Indian?"

"This land belongs to us. We were here first. Our fathers and their fathers who came before them. We don't want to be Spanish."

"Indian, we are your friends. We are going to help you. We will educate your children and build hospitals and schools and roads. We are going to give you foreign aid and give you guns and armor so you can protect yourself and be free."

"But, White Father, we are free."

"Don't argue. We know what's best for you. Now, where are the spices?"

"What spices?"

"Don't kid us, Chief. You've got to have spices around here or they wouldn't call you Indians."

"They don't call us Indians. You call us Indians. You still don't know where you are."

Columbus looked at his map again. "I've got a pretty good idea. Where is Puerto Rico from here?"

The chief pointed.

"And Cuba?"

The chief pointed again.

"Then that would put us here in the Bahamas. Why didn't I think of that before?"

"Because the season hasn't started yet. It's kind of quiet now."

Columbus said, "Well, give me all the gold you've got and I'll let you off with your lives."

"You white men are too good to us," the chief said. "How can we ever repay you?"

As Columbus stuffed the gold in the sacks he said, "Just forget about Leif the Lucky. You ever breathe a word to anyone and I'll have my boys make cement moccasins for all of you."

"Don't worry about a thing, Columbus. It will be our secret. The only one I will tell the truth to is my son."

"Where is he?"

"He's going to Yale."

EXTRY! EXTRY!

A man works hard all his life, trying to make something of himself, overcome his poverty-stricken years and achieve security and happiness. And then all of a sudden one day his son takes on a newspaper route and the man finds himself back where he started.

This happened to me awhile back. My eleven-year-old son had managed to get himself a newspaper route, but on Saturday he went off on an overnight hike with the Boy Scouts. At three o'clock on that rainy afternoon my wife informed me someone had to deliver his newspapers.

"But it's raining out," I protested. "And besides the North is playing the South in football."

"It's all right," she said, putting on her galoshes. "I'll deliver them. A little rain never hurt someone with a cold and a 101 fever."

"Okay," I said, "I'll deliver the damn papers. What really hurts is I don't even write for the paper he's delivering."

"Here's a list of the houses," my wife said. "Joel's written down the instructions as to where to get the papers and what to do."

I took the list, put on a raincoat, boots, and rain hat and went out into the pouring rain.

The truck came along at 4:30. "Where's your bag?" the driver wanted to know.

"What bag?"

"To keep your papers dry, you idiot. How many times do I have to tell you guys to bring your bag when it rains?"

"Well, you see, sir, this isn't really my route. It's my son's route. I'm just filling in for him today."

"That's a lousy excuse. Okay, keep them under your raincoat, and next time don't forget your bag."

"Yes, sir. I'll remember."

He roared off, splashing water all over my pants.

I studied the list, but it wasn't easy. Between the rain and my son's handwriting it was kind of blurred.

The first two houses didn't give me any trouble, but at the third a man came to the door. "We didn't get our paper last Friday," he said.

"That's a shame," I said. "Actually nothing much happened. You didn't miss anything."

"I'm not paying you for Friday."

"Suit yourself," I said as the rain dripped down on my face. His wife came to the door and pulled her husband away. As she closed it I heard her say, "You shouldn't yell at the poor man. It's probably the only job he could get."

In the next block a lady came to the door and said, "I forgot to pay you last week. How much is it?"

"I don't know," I said.

"Well, here's a dollar and a ten-cent tip."

"Thank you, ma'am."

"And the next time, please don't throw my paper in the bushes."

By this time the list was pretty soggy and I couldn't read it anymore, so I decided the only fair thing to do was to leave a paper at every other house until I ran out.

It worked until I came to one house where an eleven-year-old girl ran out and said, "Hey, we don't take that paper."

"It's free," I said.

"You get off our property," she said. A boxer came to the door and started growling.

I stopped running a block later.

In two hours, I had gotten rid of all the papers and was back at my house. As I soaked my feet in a pail of hot water and drank a tumbler of hot rum, the thought occurred to me that it's much easier to write for newspapers than it is to deliver them. And healthier, too.

HOW TO AUTOMATE A CIRCUS

I went to Ringling Bros. & Barnum and Bailey Circus last week with my children and was shocked to discover that in the age of automation the circus was still going along with old-fashioned, outmoded methods of operation.

As I sat there and watched the cast of more than 100 people, not to mention the people behind the scenes, I couldn't help thinking what the circus really needed was a good management consultant who could trim the manpower and make the show far more efficient.

132   *Son of the Great Society*

I can just hear him talking to John Ringling North.

"Now, Mr. North, I've made a study of your circus and you're in trouble, people-wise, that is."

"How do you mean?"

"Well, let's take the trapeze acts as an example. You've got six men and two women working two rings at the same time. I think you could cut this down to one ring, one woman, and one man."

"But you need a third man to catch the woman when she does a flip."

"You can install a computer which will be synchronized to the trapeze. It will be right where the woman artist wants it to be when she flies through the air. If it works well, you might even be able to do without the man."

"What else?"

"Well, I noticed in your lion act, five of the lions are sitting around in the cage while the sixth lion is performing. There really doesn't seem to be a need for all six lions."

"But each lion has a different trick."

"You could teach one lion all the tricks. I did a time study on them, and I discovered that for every minute they worked, the lions took three minutes doing nothing. This is a waste of lionpower."

"I don't want to argue with you, but one of the things that makes that act is that the trainer is in there with six lions. If he was only in there with one lion, there would be no danger as far as the audience is concerned."

"We could play a tape over a loudspeaker during the act which would make it sound as if there were twelve lions in the ring. Now I want to talk to you about that Siberian tiger that rides a horse."

"Don't tell me you want to get rid of the tiger?"

"No, I want to get rid of the horse. Why can't the tiger ride a wooden horse? It seems to me people are more interested in watching the tiger than the horse."

"But the whole idea is a *live* tiger is riding a *live* horse. If we make it a wooden horse, the circus fans will object."

"They will at first, but they'll get used to it. Now about those boxing bears. I think you only need one."

"How can you just have one bear fight?"

"What's the matter? Haven't you ever heard of shadow boxing?"

"What other suggestions do you have?"

"You have too many juggling acts. We have a machine

that can juggle twice as many bowling pins in half the time. We can speed up the whole operation and, at the same time, put a lot more balls in the air."

"I suppose you want me to cut down on the clowns, too?"

"I was coming to that. My study shows you can easily get by with two clowns."

"But how do you make the people laugh with just two clowns?"

"You install a laugh track over the loudspeaker system. It will sound as if you have fifty clowns."

"If it's all the same to you, I think I'll stick with what I've got now."

"That's all right with me, Mr. North. But you'd better realize we're living in a computer age, and if you keep using people in your circus, you're going to lose your shirt."

VII. COUNTDOWN

COUNTDOWN

Although it wasn't the success they hoped it would be, the biggest problem still seems to be filling time on television for space shots. When you start the event at seven in the morning and you can't get off the air even at six o'clock at night, there is a tremendous amount of padding that has to be done.

I can imagine what will happen a few space shots from now when the problem really becomes acute.

"Good morning, Chet."

"Good morning, David. How does the space shot look to you today?"

"Well, as you know, there has been a 48-hour hold on the countdown, but we expect to get the go-ahead from Houston very soon. In the meantime, let's go down to Frank McGee, who is standing by the rocket here at Cape Kennedy. Frank, can you give us some idea of what's going on down there?"

"The sun has just come up, David, and it's quite a sight to see."

"Could you describe it to us?"

"Well, from where I'm standing, it's round and looks like a great big fiery ball. Scientists have informed me it's 85 million miles from the earth and it's very hot. As you can see, it's rising from the east and it will in all probability set in the west. I have been told that without the sun the earth might not sustain life . . ."

"Can we interrupt you, Frank? We're now going to hear from Sander Vanocur, who is talking with the foreman of Wong Brothers Laundry in Cocoa Beach, the Company that has laundered all the overalls used in this space shot."

"Thanks, Chet. Mr. Wong, you've played a pretty important role in this flight. Could you tell us how exactly you washed the overalls that the technicians are using?"

"No problem. We threw them in machine, then put in water and soap. Chop-chop, they came out all clean."

"Wouldn't you say that your laundry has made a great contribution to this space flight?"

"You bet your life. If you have dirty overalls you are going to have a dirty flight."

"Thank you, Mr. Wong. Now back to Chet Huntley."

"Thanks, Sander. We're now going to Tulsa, Oklahoma, where Peter Hackes is standing by to interview a boyhood friend of astronaut Zeke Zlevin, one of the three men who will take Gemini 23 into space."

"Well, Chet, I'm here with Carlton Malabu, a boyhood friend of Zeke Zlevin's, and we've been discussing Zeke's childhood. Carl, what kind of a boy was Zeke Zlevin?"

"I really didn't know Zeke as well as I did his sister."

"What kind of a sister did Zeke have?"

"I only met her once at a dance. I didn't even know she was related to Zeke. As a matter of fact, I didn't even know Zeke had a sister."

"And that's the last time you saw Zeke?"

"Yeah. We kind of lost touch. But I always knew a guy with a sister like that would someday become an astronaut."

"David?"

"We still have some time before countdown, so let's go out to Glocking Falls where Nancy Dickerson has been talking with one of the wives of the astronauts."

"Thanks, David. It's very quiet here on Elm Street. Mrs. George Crinkle is inside this house now with her family and twelve *Life* photographers and NBC has just learned that she had a breakfast of bacon and eggs, black coffee and rye toast."

"Thanks, Nancy. Now let's go back to Frank McGee at Cape Kennedy. Frank, where is the sun now?"

"It's just over my head, Chet. And it's really getting hot. But I've just been informed that this is normal and the sun always gives off heat when it's overhead."

"Thanks, Frank. Now let's go to Houston where Ray Scherer is talking to the mother of the taxi driver who took the three astronauts to the airport."

TO PARIS AND BACK

The decision by the President to send astronauts Edward White and Charles McDivitt to Paris caught NASA officials in Houston by surprise. Although both men had orbited around the globe and one had even walked in space, no one knew how they would be able to stand up under the rigors of a full entertainment schedule in the French capital.

Medical authorities in charge of the space program voiced anxiety. One of the doctors said, "We hadn't planned on any American astronauts landing in Paris until 1967. We feel there was a great deal more to be learned before we were willing to risk the lives of these two men. Even preliminary trips around the United States by other astronauts have shown how hazardous it is for these men once they get back on the ground."

The belief here in Washington is that the President made his decision because the Russians had sent cosmonauts Titov and Gagarin to Paris and this put the Russians ahead of us in ground travel.

When the President gave his order, Houston went into action. Tracking stations all over Paris were alerted. A rescue helicopter squadron was sent to Orly Airport; the carrier *Wasp* was anchored off Le Havre.

Although McDivitt and White had trained for this trip in various officers' clubs around the country, neither one of them knew what they would be up against in Paris.

While they were suited up at Andrews Air Force Base, the two men kidded with each other. Neither showed any of the anxiety he must have felt.

The blast-off went perfectly and the men reported in to Gus Grissom that everything was A-Okay. "We're on target," White said, "and we see the Eiffel Tower off two degrees to our left."

Grissom gave them permission to make a three-day orbit around Paris.

There was a slight scare early in the trip when the astronauts got into a traffic jam at the Arc de Triomphe, and the tracking stations lost them. But by using their retro-rockets they managed to get through.

A few hours later came the toughest part of the trip. The astronauts were instructed to rendezvous at the Lido nightclub and White was to take a walk on the stage while Mc-Divitt filmed him in color.

The nation could hear every word they said.

"How is it out there?" Grissom wanted to know.

"Great," White said. "It's just beautiful up here. You've never seen anything like it."

"You dirty dog," McDivitt said, "you're clouding up my windshield."

"I think I'm losing control," White said.

"Your blood pressure seems to be rising," Grissom said anxiously.

"There's just too much to see at one time," White said. "I wish every American could be up here with me."

"You better get back now," McDivitt said.

"I'm having too much fun."

Grissom said, "That's an order, White," and White reluctantly left the stage. He said afterwards, "It was the happiest twenty minutes of my life."

When they were safely out of the nightclub, President Johnson put in a call to the men. "The nation is proud of both of you," he said. "How would you like to come down to the ranch when you come back?"

"We'd like that, sir."

"Fine, and be sure and bring those films with you."

IVAN AND MY SON

The first thought that occurred to me when I read about the Russians' space feat in March of '65 was that the American educational system had failed us again.

That night I went into my eleven-year-old son's room and said, "You better do your homework and I don't want any mistakes."

"What are you so mad at?" he asked.

"I'll tell you what I'm mad at. The Russians just put two men into space and one of them took a walk around outside the capsule."

"What's that got to do with me?"

"I'll tell you what it has to do with you. The Russians are

ahead of us in space and it's all because you American kids aren't working hard enough at your studies."

"Gee whiz," he said, "everytime the Russians put up a spaceship everyone starts yelling at us. We've got more arithmetic than we can handle as it is."

"And what do you think Ivan is saying right now?"

"Who's Ivan?"

"Ivan is your counterpart in the Soviet Union. Ivan is studying night and day to get a man on the moon, and all you're thinking about is baseball and the Boy Scouts and chewing-gum cards. I wouldn't be surprised if Ivan was laughing this very minute."

"If he has more homework than I have, I don't see what he's got to laugh about."

"That's a typical American boy's reply. But let me tell you something. It's no laughing matter when a Russian cosmonaut goes up 307 miles and gets out of his capsule and floats around for 10 minutes."

"Chuck said they didn't do it. He said the Russians can't even build a good washing machine."

"Oh, yeah? Well, Chuck doesn't know much, because these photographs show he did do it."

"Chuck says all the photographs are blurred. He says Russians even make lousy camera equipment."

"And what does Chuck say about the fact that the cosmonaut got out of his capsule and floated around?"

"He said it was probably a faulty door and the guy fell out by mistake. But Chris doesn't think so."

"What does Chris think?"

"He thinks someone forgot to put the latch on the door and so it swung out and one of the cosmonauts who doesn't like the Commie system decided it was a good chance to escape while they were flying over the United States. He says all the guy was trying to do was get away."

"Well, Chuck and Chris are both wrong," I said. "We're not going to be able to pull that stunt until 1966 and do you know why? Because you and Chuck and Chris don't know enough math."

"Holy cow," he said. "Why does it always have to be us when the Russians do something first?"

"Because we've been too easy on you. That's why.

"But all that's going to change now. We're not going to be degraded and laughed at throughout the world because you can't handle calculus in the fifth grade."

"Okay, I'll try harder," he said. "Now can I watch television?"

"That's what I mean!" I shouted. "Do you think Ivan is watching television at this moment?"

"Nope, but Chuck says they have lousy shows in Russia and there's nothing to see anyway."

THE ODD COUPLE

The announcement that the next American space flight may be for eight days was greeted with mixed reactions by those of us who worry about such things. While astronauts Mc-Divitt and White seemed to get along okay (McDivitt did call White a dirty dog for messing up his windshield), there must come a time when two men in a small capsule are going to start getting on each other's nerves.

I predict it will come around Gemini 11, when two astronauts, Major Alpha and Commander Beta, have been in orbit for twelve days.

Suddenly Alpha says to Beta, "You forgot to put the top on the food paste tube."

Beta replies, "Big deal, so I forgot. I'm getting sick and tired of you cleaning and dusting the capsule all day long."

"I happen to like a neat ship. And I don't enjoy picking up after you, either. You left your socks on the heat shelf yesterday."

"My socks were wet and I wanted them to dry. There aren't too many places you can dry socks in this thing, you know. I took this trip so I could get away from all my wife's nagging and you're getting worse than she is."

"Well, I didn't volunteer to be your maid. I've got lots of other things to worry about."

"I'm sick of your bickering. I'm going for a walk."

"Will you be back for dinner?"

"I don't know. You eat when you want to."

"Well, shut the hatch when you go out. I just cleaned the floor. And by the way, would you mind taking the garbage out?"

"Yes, I would mind. Everytime I go out you ask me to take the garbage with me."

A few hours later Commander Beta comes back.

"Where you been?" Alpha wants to know.

"What do you mean, where have I been? I told you I was taking a walk."

"Well, how do you expect me to sleep when you're out walking in space?"

"Were there any calls for me?" Beta asks.

"Your wife called."

"What did she want?"

"How do I know? I told her you weren't here."

"That was a dumb thing to say. Why didn't you tell her I was taking a walk?"

"Listen, just because we're up here together doesn't mean I have to cover for you everytime you leave the spaceship."

"Who else called?"

"The President."

"What did he want?"

"He wanted to know if we could go down to the ranch on the weekend."

"Are you going?"

"I thought I might."

"Then I'm not going. When I make my re-entry I'm not going anywhere with you."

"That goes double for me. If I never see you again it will be too soon."

"Who made up my bed?"

"I made it up."

"Listen, Alpha. If I want my bed made up I'll make it up. Do you understand?"

"I think we ought to step outside and settle this once and for all!"

"That suits me fine!"

AIRLINE RATE WAR

The U.S. airlines have been promoting all sorts of special fares lately and it's very bewildering when you're planning to take a trip, particularly since there are so many restrictions involved.

I discovered this when I called an airline the other day and said I wanted two seats to California.

"Very well. We can give you a special rate if you fly between Monday and Friday and promise not to smoke over Salt Lake City."

"I promise. What rate can I get?"

"You don't happen to be an American Indian, do you?"

"No."

"That's too bad, because if you were an American Indian and left at four o'clock in the morning and returned at three o'clock the next morning, we could give you 33⅓ percent off."

"Gee, that's too bad," I said. "Do you have any other special fares?"

"We can give you 20 percent off if you've been married for 50 years to the same person, provided you fly to California on your anniversary and return on the same day."

"That doesn't fit me. What else have you got?"

"There is our special weekend flight fare. If you're a practicing neurosurgeon going to or from a brain operation, you're entitled to a 10 percent discount."

"Neurosurgeons get all the breaks," I complained. "Don't you have any other special fares I could take advantage of?"

"Here's one," she said. "It's good from Monday evening till Wednesday noon. If you're an American Ambassador to any Scandinavian country and you're on home leave, you're entitled to first-class meals in the tourist section of the plane."

"I'm afraid I wouldn't qualify for that. Incidentally, I'm traveling with my wife."

"Well, why didn't you say so?" she said excitedly. "Is she under twenty-one years of age?"

"I'm not sure," I replied.

"Well, if she was and you both left on a weekday and neither of you had sinus conditions, you would be entitled to a discount."

"That sounds good."

"Of course, if she was pregnant and you both came from a state that didn't have an 'O' in it, you could get an extra 5 percent, unless this happened to be your first child."

"I guess that eliminates us."

"You give up too easily," she said. "Are either one of you students?"

"No."

"If you were and happened to be studying animal husbandry at a land-grant college, I could give you each 45 percent off, if you flew on Friday the 13th."

"I can't qualify for that one."

"We still have some other special discount flights," she said. "If you're a Rhodes scholar majoring in the humanities and you have a draft-deferred status and two children, you can take our coach service any time after midnight on the Fourth of July for one-third less."

"Couldn't you just make out two tickets to California at the regular rate?"

"I'm sorry," she said, "I've never made out that kind of ticket. You'll have to talk to my supervisor."

NO BIZ LIKE AIR BIZ

The entertainment on airlines has suddenly become a big and a very competitive business. Ever since TWA started showing films on their planes, every airline has tried to get in the act.

Some airlines are offering the choice of films, television, hi-fi, symphonic music, pop music, jazz, or children's stories.

One airline we flew with even showed television pictures of the takeoff and landing, which didn't thrill the lady sitting next to me as much as I thought it would.

"It gives us a chance to see the pilot make a good landing," I explained to her.

"And what are we supposed to do if we don't think he's making a good landing?"

It was something to think about.

In any case, the airlines are now in show business in a big way and no one knows where it will all end.

We must look into the future a few years and find ourselves at a board meeting of Twentieth Century-Fox Airlines, presided over by Sol Hurok, the chairman of the board.

"Gentlemen," Mr. Hurok says, "our earnings are down. Do you know why?"

"We showed *John Goldfarb* on that Notre Dame alumni charter flight?" a vice-president suggests.

"No, that's not what hurt us," Hurok says. "The competition is killing us. People are getting tired of watching movies, listening to hi-fi and tuning in children's stories. They want something different."

"But," the public relations man says, "we've got Harry Belafonte on our New York-to-Miami run—live."

"Sure," says Hurok, "and as soon as we did, Braniff booked the Beatles and took all the teen-age business away."

"I don't think it was the Beatles that hurt us as much as Delta Airlines booking Sonny Liston and Cassius Clay to fight daily on their Chicago-New Orleans flight."

"Okay, so we're not appealing to the sports fans," Hurok says. "But we gave them Margot Fonteyn and Nureyev on the shuttle to Washington and we still lost business."

"That's because American Airlines was featuring Van Cliburn and Artur Rubinstein—at the same time."

"You never know what will work and what won't," the sales manager says. "United Airlines had *After the Fall* and they did no business at all."

"People who fly want to be uplifted. *Hello, Dolly!* is packing them in on Pan American."

"Sure, but take Carol Channing off the plane and see what happens to their business."

Hurok says, "I'll admit we made mistakes. Booking the Vienna Boys Choir to play on the Las Vegas jet was an error, but why didn't we do any business when we had the *Holiday on Ice* show on the Puerto Rico run?"

"The aisles were too narrow," the chief pilot says, "and most of the passengers didn't know the cast was on skates."

"Well," says Hurok, "we've got to come up with something new."

A vice-president raises his hand. "I know this is going to shock you, but I think we can offer our passengers something that no other airline has."

"What's that?"

"Silence. No movies, no shows, no hi-fi, no television. The passengers can read a book or sleep or just sit and think. It will be the biggest attraction to come along in years."

"It's great," shouts the advertising manager. "But will the CAB approve? If we offer silence, they'll accuse us of unfair competition."

"He's right," says Hurok. "Now, I've just made a deal with the Esther Williams Aquacade."

VIII. GOOD NEWS
IS NO NEWS

007 AND THE GOP

James Bond kissed the delectable Miss Moneypenny on the forehead and walked into M's office. M lit up his pipe and then said, "007, I'm sending you on the most dangerous assignment you've ever tackled. I want you to go to the Republican National Headquarters in Washington, D.C., and get a copy of the list of people who contributed more than $1,000 to the Barry Goldwater campaign in 1964. I can't impress on you how important this mission is. If the list falls into the wrong hands it will mean the end of the two-party system in America."

Bond took the next plane out and landed at Dulles Airport at 10:30 in the evening. A tall brunette in a Sting Ray met him and drove him into town. "Daddy couldn't meet you," she said. "He had to go to San Francisco to address the United Nations."

Bond smirked as they got into the car and then he leaned over as if to kiss her. But just as he got his arms around her a Secret Service man popped up from the back and said, "Easy, Charlie, you're not fooling around with Tiffany Case."

"Oh, phooey," said the brunette and then she angrily put the car into gear.

The Sting Ray dropped Bond off at the Republican National Headquarters. It was dark as 007 climbed the fire escape behind the building.

He jimmied open the window, parted the curtains, and jumped into the office of the Republican Treasurer. As he walked toward the desk he was struck over the head and went down on the carpet. When he came to he was looking into the business end of a .45.

"Who are you with?" the man behind the .45 said.

"I'm just a volunteer for William Buckley," Bond said. "And who are you?"

"I'm with the American Conservatives For Conservative America," the man said. "And I think you're after what I'm after."

Suddenly the door was thrown open and a man said, "Drop it." He was carrying an Italian semi-automatic Beretta.

The ACFCA man dropped his .45.

The Beretta man said, "Where's the list?"

"We don't know. Who are you with?"

"I'm with the Young Republicans For a Young Republic and once we get that list we're going to take over the party."

"Not while we're alive," said a man holding a Thompson submachine gun at the window. "Drop that Beretta."

"Who is he?" Bond asked the ACFCA man.

"He's with the Free Society For a Free Society. One of Barry's boys."

The FSFFS man didn't see someone come from behind him and knock the machine gun out of his hands.

"I've got a hand grenade here and I'll pull the pin if anyone moves."

"It's the Moderate Republicans For Moderation," someone gasped.

Bond thought fast. "Before blood is shed, did any of you know there is a copy of *Choice,* the film made by the Mothers For a Moral America?" he asked.

"Where?" everyone wanted to know.

"In the filing cabinet over there."

They all rushed to the cabinet. "There's a projector over here," someone yelled.

While everyone was watching the salacious movie, Bond managed to break open the desk drawer of the Republican Treasurer and grab the list. Then, while the others watched a girl in a topless bathing suit, Bond dashed out of the door. They didn't even realize he was gone.

Later Bond delivered the list to the brunette in the Sting Ray. "Give it to your daddy to give to Senator Dirksen."

"Oh, 007, you saved the two-party system. How can we ever thank you?" the brunette said.

Bond looked back at the Secret Service man and shrugged his shoulders.

THE FELLOW TRAVELER

The State Department has told its passport offices around the country to do nothing that might in any way encourage Americans to travel abroad while the nation suffers from a gold drain. The offices were also told to take down any posters or other displays that might encourage foreign travel.

The scene is a passport office in New York City. A man comes to the desk and says to the woman behind the counter, "I'm a tourist. I need a passport."

The woman presses a button with her foot, alerting four FBI men in an adjoining room.

The woman says, "What did you want a passport for?

"Were you planning to use it to go abroad?"

"No, I wanted it to paste my green stamps in. Sure, I want to go abroad!"

"We can't stop you from getting a passport. All we can do is warn you about the cholera epidemic and let you make your own decision."

"What cholera epidemic?"

"I'm sorry, I can't give out any tourist information. Please fill this out. I presume you have riot insurance?"

"No. I don't have riot insurance. What do I need riot insurance for?"

"We find it's very helpful, especially if you plan on visiting an American embassy."

"Look, I just want to take a vacation with my family."

"You mean you were going to travel with your dependents at a time like this?"

"What do you mean, a time like this? I hear it's safer in Berlin than on a subway in New York City."

"Very well, let me have the names of your next of kin."

The man gives her the information.

The woman says, "You understand, of course, this passport can protect you only in countries where we have diplomatic relations. It doesn't cover you for floods, hurricanes, or tornadoes."

"I wasn't thinking about floods, hurricanes, or tornadoes."

"We're asking all Americans to think about them."

"I was going to Switzerland."

"During the avalanche season?"

"Oh, for crying out loud! Are you going to give me the passport or aren't you?"

"Our instructions are to issue passports to anyone who wants them, regardless of his political beliefs."

"You don't even know my political beliefs."

"We have a good idea of the type of person who wants to travel abroad at this time. We call him a fellow traveler."

"This is nonsense. I'm a businessman, a registered Republican, and I want to show my family Europe. Is there anything subversive about that?"

"Why don't you take them to Disneyland?"

"I've been to Disneyland."

"Since they added the submarine ride?"

"Can I have my passport?"

"Just a moment, please." She goes in to consult the FBI men.

"Give him the passport," the chief advises. "We'll get him at Kennedy Internatonal Airport when we can pick up the entire family at the same time."

COLDFINGER

Industrial espionage, or the art of spying on other American companies, has become a multimillion-dollar business. A *Harvard Business Review* survey revealed that industrial espionage was discovered by 27 percent of all the companies interviewed, and everyone admitted it was on the increase.

It opens up a whole new world for spies.

Harvey Sickles, agent 8½, is having tea with his superior, Mr. X.

"8½, this could be your most dangerous case. The Coldfinger Capsule Co. has just perfected a new pill that will give people six months of relief from one cold. The Impact Pill people have to have the formula or they'll be destroyed. I don't care how you get the secret, but I want it here by Monday."

"I've got you, chief."

"Be careful, 8½. Coldfinger's a killer. He has a nose spray that is worse than anything they've been using in Vietnam."

The next evening Sickles arrives at the apartment of Miss

Mairsy Doats, a luscious, pouting blonde intimate of the famous spy.

Sickles takes her in his arms.

"Don't kiss me, darling. I've got a cold," she says huskily.

"Why do you think I'm here?" Sickles says, before pressing his lips on hers.

He kisses her for a full minute. Mairsy Doats swoons. "Let me get into something more comfortable."

"I can't, baby," Sickles says, sneezing. "I'm on a case."

He leaves the perplexed Mairsy Doats on the couch, jumps into his Aston-Marton and drives to the laboratory of the Coldfinger Capsule Co. A light is on in the laboratory, and Dr. Felicia Oomph is bent over her microscope.

Sickles enters and the doctor, startled, looks up. "What do you want?"

"I'm a man and you're a woman," Sickles says, not wanting to frighten her. "I want to ask you one question, Doctor. Have you ever been kissed by a man, really kissed?"

The doctor takes off her glasses, and she's beautiful.

"No, I never have. I'm afraid of men."

"Why?"

"Because of their germs. Men carry around millions and millions of germs."

"But I love you," Sickles says.

"I love you, too," Dr. Oomph says, pressing his hand. "But you've got a cold, and I'm afraid."

"Perhaps you could give me something for it, and then I could kiss you."

"The only thing I have is $C1H306N7$. It won't cure the cold, but it will give you instant relief. Here, take one now and one every six months."

"Thank you, Felicia. Gosh, I feel like a new man."

"You can kiss me now," Dr. Oomph says.

He kisses her. Then he pretends to blow his nose. The ordinary handkerchief is a secret radio transmitter, and Sickles broadcasts the formula to Mr. X.

Dr. Oomph starts taking off her smock, but Mr. X says, "Return immediately, 8½. We need you on a toothpaste case right away."

GOOD NEWS IS NO NEWS

There were a lot of red faces in Washington because of last summer's contretemps with the Prime Minister of Singapore, Lee Kuan Yew, who revealed in a press interview that he was offered a bribe of $3 million to hush up an American CIA fiasco in 1961. Mr. Lee said he indignantly refused the money because he and his party couldn't be bribed, but he would consider an offer of $33 million instead.

The State Department denied the incident had ever taken place, so Mr. Lee produced a letter of apology written by Secretary of State Dean Rusk to him. Rusk said there had been a misunderstanding over the denial, which, whether they liked it or not, confirmed Prime Minister Lee's story.

Among the red faces I saw was one belonging to the Enchiladan Ambassador to the United States, who was dining alone at the Sans Souci.

I asked him why he was so upset.

"I am in trouble with my government because of Singapore."

"How is that? Singapore is not in South America."

"You do not understand. Four years ago there came to my country one of your CIA people who offered to bribe one of our officials for information about our government. He was arrested and thrown into jail. A few weeks later a high official from your government came to me and asked me how much it would cost to get him out of jail.

"I said $5,000. They offered $3,500, and I recommended to my country we take it. Now I am in trouble because they have read in the paper that the Singapore government was offered $3 million if they would release the CIA man there. My government is very angry with me because we sold out so cheaply."

"I should think they would be," I said.

"I am very disappointed with your State Department. We have always been very good friends of the United States and we should have got the going rate for CIA agents."

"But no one had put a price on a CIA agent before. It wasn't your fault."

"That's what I told my government. But they said this is

typical of American policy in Latin America. They will pay
$3 million to hush up a scandal in the Far East but only
$3,500 to hush up one in Latin America. What kind of an
Alliance for Progress is this?"

"Did anyone offer you an explanation?"

"They told me that the CIA agent in Singapore was mixed
up with a girl and that's why they had to pay more."

"But $3 million! She must have been some girl!"

"That's exactly what I was thinking. We have some beautiful women in our country, but $3 million—the mind bog-
gles."

"What are you planning to do about it?"

"We are going to bring it up at the next OAS meeting. We
are going to tell the United States that they can send all the
CIA agents they want into Latin America, but they will have
to pay $3 million for each one that gets caught. We can't cut
our prices lower than Singapore."

"Did you tell Dean Rusk about it?"

"I wrote him a letter, but his secretary wrote back and said
Mr. Rusk has decided not to write letters anymore—to anybody."

"It's probably a good policy," I agreed.

The Ambassador got up to leave. "It's now up to the
United States. Do you realize 100 inept CIA agents could resolve our balance of payments problem for two years?"

A FUNNY THING HAPPENED ON THE . . .

The Egyptian newspaper *Al Gumhurriya* charged that the
U.S. Central Intelligence Agency is trying to "dominate
Egypt and the whole Arab world." The paper said the CIA
was not planting rumors but "inventing jokes against the
state."

This is the first time that any reference has been made to
the CIA's role in planting jokes in foreign countries, and now
that the secret is out, I no longer feel any restraint in writing
about it.

The U.S. Bureau of Jokes is a separate branch of the CIA,
and is so powerful that its existence is unknown to everyone
except four or five top American officials who pride themselves on having a sense of humor.

The head of the department is Horace Glum, and he was kind enough to speak to me, provided I gave his side of what happened at the Bay of Pigs—jokewise, that is.

Glum told us that all jokes for CIA infiltration work are thought up in Washington and then sent out to his agents by code. The punch lines are sent separately, so in case the code is broken the joke is still protected.

"Suppose," said Glum, "we wanted to bring down a dictator in South America. We would send a joke to one of our agents and he would go to a bazaar or a café and say to a native, 'Did you hear the one about Dictator Gonzalez? He fell into the river and was saved by a peasant. The Dictator was so grateful he told the peasant he would do anything he could for him, and the peasant replied, "There is only one thing you can do for me. Don't tell anyone I saved you." '

"In two weeks the story will have made the rounds of the country and in three weeks Gonzalez will be thrown out on his ear."

"Have you ever used that story in actual practice?"

"We've brought down three governments with it so far, though I must admit it's getting to be quite a chestnut."

"What was the biggest success your department ever had?"

"Well, we came up with quite a good one a few years ago. It was a joke about Mao Tse-tung. He sent a telegram to Khrushchev saying 'China starves. Please send food.' Khrushchev replied to Mao, 'Tighten your belts.' Mao replied to Khrushchev, 'Please send belts.'

"Our agent planted this story in Peking in hopes of toppling Mao, but the Chinese were very smart and they planted the story in Moscow. In two weeks, instead of Mao, Khrushchev was out! Surprised the hell out of all of us here."

"What was the one you planted that got the Egyptians so mad?"

"I'm not sure. We've planted so many there. I think it may have been the one about a newspaperman fleeing the United Arab Republic. A friend asked him why. 'There are two reasons,' the newspaperman said, 'First, the regime might change and all my friends will be killed.' 'That's impossible,' the friend said. The newspaperman replied, 'I told you I have two reasons.' "

"That got to them?" I said.

"When it hits Aswan, I don't give Nasser two more months."

"What about the Bay of Pigs?"

"We had some pretty good jokes to send in, but President Kennedy wouldn't give us any air cover for them. By the time we got the jokes on the beach, the show was over."

"Do you think Cuba is lost to the free world?"

"I'm not too sure. What do you think of this one? Three guys are in prison in Havana. One says he's there because he was against Che Guevara. The other says he's there because he was for Che Guevara. The third man finally speaks up and says, 'I'm Che Guevara.' "

I smiled. "If I was Castro, I'd resign."

IS THERE A RED CHINA?

One of the most astounding discoveries in history was made the other day when a group of American State Department people found a new country named Red China. For years there had been rumors that there was a country in the Far East with a population of 800 million people. Yet no one in the United States would believe it.

But an expedition of Senators led by Marco Fulbright came across it accidentally while looking for a new route to North Vietnam.

When the existence of Red China was reported, a meeting of all the top policy people in the State Department was called.

"If this is true," said one of the Assistant Secretaries, "that means the world is round."

"Hogwash," said another Secretary. "We all know there is a country called China already, so how could there be another China? Look at our maps. China is right here in the Formosa Strait."

"That's right," a Secretary said. "And our maps are all up to date."

"What's that large land mass across the water from it?" someone asked.

"It's marked 'unexplored.' "

"Perhaps that's where Red China is."

"I'm an old China hand, and I say there is no place called Red China. The only China is located on the island of Formosa."

"What proof do we have that there really is a country with

800 million people in it, except for the word of a few disgruntled Senators?" an Undersecretary demanded. "They're only trying to discredit our foreign policy anyway."

"There is no proof," a Far East expert said, "except the West Germans have announced they plan to build a $150 million steel mill there. I don't think they'd put in that kind of money if the country didn't exist."

The Secretary of State spoke up. "That is a point. The only thing I can't understand is how we could have missed it all these years."

"Perhaps there is a cloud cover over it all the time," someone suggested.

"Does the CIA have anything on it?"

"No, sir. They're as much in the dark as we are. The French, the British, and the Canadians have all reported that they believe there is a Red China, but the Russians now claim it isn't there."

The old China hand spoke up. "Mr. Secretary, I believe we're only looking for trouble by following up the rumor. We already have a China. It's *our* kind of China. Another China would only mean trouble."

"But," said one of the other men, "if the reports are true that this land mass contains 800 million people, won't we have to deal with it sooner or later? I think we should announce that we don't believe there is a Red China, but if there is, we intend to contain it, but not isolate it."

The Secretary of State said, "That's a good phrase, 'containment but not isolation.' I think I'll use it in my next press conference. Our only problem is that if we admit there is such a place, we might be forced to admit her into the United Nations."

"Precisely, sir," a Secretary spoke out. "Besides, we've told the American people for seventeen years that there is no Red China. If we admit there is a Red China now, we would only confuse them."

One of the advisers said, "Seventeen years ago, the American people didn't believe in flying saucers, either. Perhaps we could announce the existence of Red China and flying saucers at the same time."

NO TROUBLE IN ZEMULULU

I just received a very heartbreaking letter from a friend of mine who happens to be the American Ambassador to an African country which, to protect him, I will call Zemululu.

He writes that he is in serious trouble with the State Department and doesn't know what to do about it.

His problems first began when a year went by without any anti-American demonstrations in the country. Washington became suspicious and thought he was keeping something from them. He received a cable which said, "Can't understand lack of anti-American demonstrations your area. Please clarify why natives are friendly."

My friend wired back he had no explanation for it unless the country's climate did not lend itself to demonstrating. He thought he would hear no more from Washington, but a week later he received a follow-up cable: "How come you have sent in no reports on coups or attempted coups in your country? You only Ambassador in Africa not expecting a revolution. What have you been doing?"

He replied, "Zemululu not coup-conscious. Military getting along fine with premier."

By now the matter was being given serious study by the African hands in the State Department. A cable was dispatched: "You have failed to keep us informed on racial tension. How much is there and when is it likely to explode?"

His reply was a weak, "No racial tension in sight and our people not expecting any. Please advise what I'm doing wrong."

There was an ominous silence for a few weeks, but then he had a bit of good luck and was able to wire: "Peace Corps scandal may be brewing upcountry. Could cause tremendous damage to our relations here."

They immediately cabled back, "Good boy. This may be the first break we've had. Send us full details."

After a thorough investigation he replied, "Peace Corps scandal turned out to be false alarm. First report indicated Peace Corps volunteer was going to have a baby, but corrected transmission says Peace Corps volunteer delivered a baby. Sorry to get your hopes up."

State was very annoyed. To top it off they sent him a nasty

wire saying, "Your AID operation has just been audited and found to be completely in order. There has been no misuse of funds or hint of black market operation. AID perplexed and thinking of cutting off money."

The Ambassador replied, "Please tell AID not to act too hastily. While American money being kept from profiteers at moment, situation could change overnight."

A month went by and suddenly the code machines started clicking again. "Congressional junket just returned from Zemululu reports they pleased with stability and progress made there and very impressed with lack of subversion. Do you realize this could hurt overall budget for upcoming year? Also understand *Time* and *Newsweek* correspondents have made official complaints to their editors that Zemululu is dead as running story. Everyone here very depressed."

To save his job the Ambassador wired back, "Two Chinese cultural attachés have just arrived from Peking, and have opened Chinese restaurant."

An immediate reply from Washington said, "Congratulations. All of us here delighted with news. How many CIA men can we send you?"

RED ALERT

Not long ago the television networks played a dirty trick on the American public. NBC and CBS both pre-empted their regular shows because of the Gemini 8 flight, which had gotten into trouble and had to be returned to earth in an emergency splashdown. All the networks received angry telephone calls from viewers who felt they were being cheated out of their regular evening entertainment.

The American Broadcasting Company was the only one who showed some consideration for its audience by putting on *Batman*, the most important program in its stable, despite the Gemini emergency. But even ABC let the public down, by interrupting *Batman* with bulletins. This engendered the wrath of *Batman* fans all over the country.

It gives one great faith in the American people, and shows the power of entertainment over news in TV programming.

If the balloon ever went up something like this could happen.

"We interrupt this program to announce that a large fleet of unidentified bomber aircraft is now heading toward the United States and the entire Air Force Defense Command has been put on alert."

An indignant viewer gets through to NBC. "What do you mean interrupting *The Virginian* for a lousy news bulletin? If you don't put the regularly scheduled program back on the air, your Nielsen rating is really going to suffer."

The announcer continues, "The bombers coming in from the East are believed to be the type carrying atomic weapons. All SAC planes are in the air."

A caller at CBS says, "I want to speak to Bill Paley. How dare your network substitute a news special for *Lost in Space*? What am I supposed to tell my kids?"

"The President of the United States is meeting now with the National Security Council. In the meantime Polaris submarines have been put on station and all missiles have been ordered armed."

ABC's switchboard is flooded with callers. "You finks. Your guy came on just when Batman and Robin were about to be crushed to death in a cement mixer. Get that news bum off the air or I'm going to write my Congressman."

"The planes are now two hours and fifteen minutes away from Newfoundland and are still heading straight for the North American continent. All ICBM units are on *red* alert. This is not, repeat, not a test."

"Let me speak to David Brinkley, operator. He's ruined my evening and I would just like to give him a piece of my mind. A guy works all day and wants a little relaxation and all they give us is news bulletins."

"But, sir, there may be an attack on the United States."

"That's not my problem. Why don't you people stick to *TV Guide* like you're supposed to? I want to see the Bob Hope Special."

Over at CBS a caller is screaming into the phone, "I want to know if you're going to put on the *Dick Van Dyke* show or not. If you're not I want to go to bed. I haven't missed the *Dick Van Dyke* show since it's been on the air and you people better realize the American public is sick and tired of being pushed around. Why don't you leave the news to the educational TV stations?"

"We have just had a late bulletin that the enemy planes have turned back. They are returning to their bases. The President has called off the SAC bombers."

"Is this the CBS operator? Well you just tell your people

there that the next time they pre-empt the *Beverly Hillbillies* for an air raid, I'm going to write directly to the sponsors. Now what do you have to say about that?"

THE UNHAPPY AFRICAN

The Prime Minister of Zemululu was in Washington last week, and as the leader of the only democracy left in Africa, he has been very much criticized in diplomatic circles and at the United Nations.

I was fortunate to have a few moments alone with him.

"Sir, how do you explain the fact that you are the only democracy left in Africa?"

"I have a weak army," he said sadly.

"I'm sorry to hear that," I said.

"That is one of the reasons I have come to the United States. I hope to get military aid so I can beef up my armed forces. Once the army is strong enough, I'm sure they'll want to overthrow the government. Then I can retire to Switzerland. The climate in my country is abominable."

"Mr. Prime Minister, there has been much criticism of your form of government in international circles. No one can understand how a country of your size and your potential can still allow free elections and permit opposition parties to flourish."

"What people don't realize is that we're a young nation that was under colonial rule for a very long time. We would welcome military rule in a minute if we knew how to achieve it. We haven't chosen freedom because we wanted it. At the time it seemed the only way out of our dilemma. Someday, when we get on our feet, we hope to have a dictatorship like everyone else in Africa, but it takes time."

"In your inauguration speech of 1965 you promised to do away with free elections and to exile all the opposition parties. Why haven't you fulfilled these promises?"

"Because, if I did that, I would be playing into the hands of the opposition. There is nothing the opposition wants more than to be exiled. The climate in my country is something fierce."

"Mr. Prime Minister, one of the big fears in the West is that, in a democracy such as yours, there is always a chance of a Communist take-over. This is one of the reasons why the West feels much more secure with a military dictatorship. What guarantees do we have that under your system the Communists won't win an election?"

"We've tried to get the Communists to take over, but they've refused. They keep saying, 'Who wants to rule a country with such an unhealthy climate?' "

"What do you see in the future for Zemululu?"

"We have to produce a strong officer corps, which will become discontented very easily. It is my hope that we can train enough officers abroad so, as soon as they return, they will start plotting against the government. This will take time. We should have started the program much earlier. I also need tanks, a few airplanes, and one fully equipped armored regiment. Without the equipment the most militant officers could never pull off a coup."

"And you hope to arrange all this while you're in the United States?"

"They've provided this for other African countries. I don't see any reason why they would turn me down."

"Suppose they refuse to help you?"

"My people are getting fed up with democracy. We have a right to a military government like everybody else. If we don't get help from the United States, we will take the matter to the United Nations. Even a UN Trusteeship would be better than what we've got now."

"How long will you stay in Washington?"

"As long as I can. I hate to go back to that lousy climate."

SEX AND THE SINGLE NATION

Canada can now be considered a major power. She rates it because she has a major sex scandal. This means more in the world of power politics than the highest stockpile of hydrogen bombs.

No country which wants to play a deciding role in international affairs can have any influence without a first-class sex-in-government crisis. France found this out when she had the "Ballet Rose." Britain discovered it when it produced the Profumo affair and the United States became a first-class nation only after the Bobby Baker case came to light.

Russia is working on a crash program to catch up with the West, and its leaders predict they'll have an earth-shaking sex scandal about 1967. The Communist Chinese, who got started late, are not expected to have a major sex scandal for at least 10 years.

What this has done for Canada in terms of morale and spirit has been unbelievable. When the Minister of Justice announced in Parliament that Canada had a sex scandal that could be worse than the Profumo affair, the country went wild. Factory workers were dismissed, banks closed, schools were let out, and everyone poured into the streets, kissing and slapping each other on the back.

Crowds gathered around television store fronts, hoping some of the details would be shown on TV. Other crowds gathered in front of newspaper offices where editors read bulletins to the happy throngs.

"We're on the front pages of every newspaper in the world," a man shouted, and the people cheered.

"We're asking for a veto in the United Nations," another man yelled.

"Gerda Munsinger, the German woman in the affair, says she'll come back and tell all!" someone else yelled.

The people could not contain themselves. Some laughed; a few cried for joy.

At the Toronto stock exchange the Canadian dollar, which had been soft, was suddenly in demand.

And in Ottawa telegrams of congratulations from all over the world poured in. One leader cabled, "Thank God you got it before the Cubans."

But after all the celebrations, the Canadians started sobering up. A spokesman for the government said, "To have your own sex scandal is a very sobering responsibility. We can't use it as a club against a non-sex scandal nation. It must be used for peaceful purposes only."

There has been no official word yet as to how Washington is taking its neighbor's good fortune.

One U.S. Canada-watcher told me: "We don't know how big the sex scandal will be, so we can't guess how it will affect United States–Canadian relations. Of course, we're happy for them, and we'll help them in any way we can."

"Does that mean you'd be willing to pool your sex scandal resources?"

"I didn't say that. I think that's something for NATO to decide."

IX. KISS ME, STUPID

KISS ME, STUPID

A Florida dentist named Dr. Doran D. Zimmer has discovered, after a five-year research program, that cavities can be caused by kissing. The results of his studies, which were financed by a grant from the United States Public Health Service, have thrown the dental profession into a tizzy and could change the kissing habits of the country.

It is too early to know what effect the results will have on kissing in the United States, but a spot survey I made shows that people are really worried about it.

I called my own dentist and asked him if it was okay to continue kissing, now that the scientific facts had been established.

He replied, "It's all right to go ahead, provided you brush your teeth before and after each kiss."

I pointed out that this might cause some consternation in the circles I travel in.

"It's your teeth," he said, "and all I can do is warn you of the consequences."

"Is there anything else I can do?"

"The Eskimos rub noses and their teeth are excellent. Have you ever thought of that?"

"I did once, but I caught a cold," I said.

After I hung up, I called a teen-age daughter of a friend of mine and asked her if the kids had been affected by the news.

"We had an experiment in our class," she said. "Half the kids necked and the other half didn't, and the half that didn't had 25 percent fewer cavities than the kids that did."

"Well, there's a lot to be said, then, for not kissing," I told her. "The kids that didn't neck didn't have to go to the dentist, and that must have saved their parents a lot of money."

162

"Not really. Because the kids that didn't neck had to go to psychiatrists instead."

I made another call to a toothpaste manufacturer, who said that as soon as the news broke, his research people got on it right away.

"We're working on a new toothpaste for people who kiss a lot but can only brush once a day. It's called 'Lust' and the minute your teeth come in contact with another person's teeth, it kills all the germs in both your mouths."

"It sounds like a breakthrough," I said excitedly.

"We're very high on it. Our entire advertising campaign next year is going to be to fight 'smooch decay.'"

I finally called someone connected with the government and asked if they were going to propose any legislation to prohibit kissing in the United States.

"We can't stop Americans from kissing," he said, "but we think the government should at least warn people what they're getting into."

"Is there any truth to the rumor that the government will demand warning labels on perfumes that induce kissing?" I asked him.

"It's being considered. We would prefer to find something to add to the drinking water which could protect everybody. But so far we haven't come up with anything, so we'll have to stick with an educational campaign. We believe that people who have been kissing for years won't be able to stop. But perhaps those who are just starting out will realize the damage it can do to their teeth and will take up cigarette smoking instead."

SUBVERSIVES FOR MEDICARE

One of the provisions of Medicare is that any person not covered by Social Security or railroad retirement insurance is ineligible for hospital and nursing home benefits if he is a Communist or a member of a Communist front.

To enforce this, a person in this category must answer the following questions: "Are you now or have you during the past 12 months been a member of any organization which is required to register under the Internal Security Act of 1950 as a Communist action organization, a Communist front organization, or a Communist-infiltrated organization?"

I hadn't realized what chaos this question was causing until I got a call from my Uncle Harry, who was all excited about it.

"How are you, Uncle Harry?" I asked.

"My rheumatism is killing me. That's what I'm calling about. What is all this business about not being a member of the Communist party or a Communist-infiltrated organization in order to get Medicare?"

"It's quite simple, Uncle Harry. We don't want people who would overthrow our government to get free hospital and nursing care."

"With my rheumatism I can't even get to the doctor, much less overthrow the government."

"Ah, Uncle Harry, that's just it. If you were a Communist and you got hospital care, you might become well, and then you *would* be in a position to overthrow the government."

"If I could get rid of my rheumatism, I'd be willing to join the John Birch Society."

"But, Uncle Harry, I don't know what you're all excited about. You're not a member of the Communist party, are you?"

"I should hope not. Have you ever seen anyone with rheumatism who wanted to be part of a sit-in?"

"Then what are you worried about?"

"It's these Communist-front and Communist-infiltrated organizations. I don't know if I belong to any or not."   .

"Well, what organizations have you joined in the past 12 months?"

"The Bideaway Village for Senior Citizens, $10 down and $10 a month."

"I'm sure that's not on the subversive list."

"What about the Retired Friends of the Forest Hills Library?"

"That I'd better check. Anything else?"

"The Planned Parenthood Association?"

"That sounds bad, Uncle Harry. It's not on the list now, but you never can tell."

"I knew it," Uncle Harry said. "I'll never get my rheumatism cured."

"Now don't be discouraged, Uncle Harry. This law is only aimed at bad old people, not good old people. I'm sure they didn't have you in mind when they wrote it."

"At your age you can say that. If you want my opinion, I think the government's trying to save some money."

"Uncle Harry, you don't seem to understand. The United States is out to eradicate the Communist party. If their members don't get hospital care, they'll be eradicated that much sooner."

"Now that you explain it to me, it does make sense. I have only one problem."

"What's that?"

"With my rheumatism my hands shake so much I can't even answer 'No' to the question."

THE BEAUTY OF SCIENCE

It has just been reported to a group of American physicists that a new "gravity bomb," equal to one million H-bombs, could someday be built. At the moment it is impractical because of size and cost, as well as a lack of a triggering device, but they said the H-bomb was impractical a few years ago, too.

The important thing is that in the next 10 years many countries will be developing atomic bombs and H-bombs and the countries that now possess these bombs will no longer have the prestige and position they hold in world affairs today.

Therefore, the gravity bomb could be the answer to those who want to stay ahead in the nuclear arms race.

The big fear in the world today is that China, France, Israel, Egypt, India, and Monaco may all become nuclear powers. And the question is, how do you settle disputes when everyone has an H-bomb?

The answer is the gravity bomb. No country is going to start any trouble with us when they know that if they use the H-bomb, we would use a bomb one million times more powerful.

The only two nations who have the capacity to build the gravity bomb are the United States and the Soviet Union. But the fear is that if one country gets its gravity bomb built first, the other country might feel endangered. The best way to resolve this is for the United States, who will probably get its bomb built first, to allow the Soviet Union to steal its secrets.

This could easily be done by inviting Dr. Klaus Fuchs back to the U.S. to work on our bomb. Dr. Fuchs would pass on the secret to the Russians who would then develop their own gravity bomb, and the balance of power in the world would be saved.

It is possible that some way would have to be worked out to dramatize the effectiveness of the "G" bomb. Since you couldn't very well test it on the earth, the best way to show people the power of the bomb might be to blow up the moon. Everyone could see it and we don't really need the moon much anyway.

Because of its size and power, the United States and the Soviet Union would have to reassure the non-gravity-bomb nations that they would only use the "G" bomb as a last resort, if the other side used it first. We could still fight small wars with H-bombs, but only a madman would think of getting into a war with the "G" bomb.

There will be a great deal of pressure from our allies for their own stockpile of "G" bombs, but it would be a mistake for us to give in to them, just as it would be a mistake for the Russians to turn over their "G" bomb to the Chinese.

France and China might threaten to build their own "G" bombs, but scientists believe it would take them at least ten years to develop them. By this time we will have discovered the "F" bomb which will be one million times more powerful than the "G" bomb.

So, even if the other countries do eventually find out the secret of the "G" bomb, they still will not possess the ultimate weapon. That is the beauty of science.

A MERRY DR. SPOCK

Dr. Spock, America's leading authority on children, has come up with some revolutionary ideas for Christmas. He says that the holiday season is so overdone that children go to pieces under the tension, and he warns that Christmas exploits and fosters children's naturally greedy tendencies.

To solve the problem, the good doctor thinks we should do away with mass family gatherings and visits, that we should leave children home when shopping, that they should be shielded from live Santas, and that a child should be limited to only one or, at the most, two Christmas presents.

The scene is Christmas morning. A ten-year-old child comes running down the stairs in his pajamas while his parents sit nervously by the Christmas tree.

There are two packages under the tree. The boy rips them both open. "Oh, boy," he cries, "an Erector set and a pair of galoshes." He starts looking behind the tree. "Where's the other stuff?" he asks.

The mother says, "That's all there is, son."

"All there is?" the boy says. "But it's Christmas."

"We know that, son," the father says. "But Dr. Spock says you should only get one or, at the most, two Christmas presents this year."

"Who's Dr. Spock?"

"He is a very famous pediatrician and he writes books on how to raise children. He says the more presents we buy you, the more chance you have of going to pieces on Christmas Day."

The boy says, "He must be some kind of a nut."

"He is not a nut. He is a very distinguished man who knows what goes on in the minds of children."

"Well, if he's not a nut, he's a fink," the boy cries. "What kind of a Christmas is this, anyway?"

"Dr. Spock is just trying to keep your greedy tendencies in check. He says the less we give you, the happier you will be."

The boy screams, "I'm not greedy. I only want what's coming to me."

"But if we gave you everything you wanted, you would just go to pieces. We don't want you to have a nervous breakdown."

"What's a nervous breakdown?"

"It's when you get sick and depressed."

"But I'm sick and depressed now."

"Yes, but you would be much worse if you got a lot of presents."

"I'm going to tell Grandma this afternoon," the boy says.

"She's not coming over this afternoon," the mother tells the son.

"Why not?"

"Because Dr. Spock doesn't believe in mass family gatherings at Christmas time. He says it will only unnerve you. The three of us are going to spend a quiet day together."

"Without any toys?"

"We'll sing Christmas carols," the father says.

"What am I going to tell all my friends when they ask me what I got for Christmas?" the boy asks.

"Tell them you may not have material things, but mentally you're much better off than they are."

"They'll never believe it," the boy says. "I think I'm having a nervous breakdown." He begins to cry and won't stop.

The father says, "Now, calm down while your mother opens her two presents."

"Two presents?" The mother starts weeping. "I thought Dr. Spock was only talking about children."

The father says, "I never saw so many people go to pieces in my life."

THE LIGHT THAT FAILED

It apparently doesn't pay to hold your breath waiting for an explanation as to why all the lights in the Northeast part of the United States and Canada went out last November. Many fanciful versions of what happened have been given, but the reason no one will know the real truth is that the computers involved are not talking.

As with the medical profession, there is an ethical question involved, and no computer would ever testify against another computer, no matter how guilty the computer happened to be.

But from an unimpeachable power source this column was able to learn that the breakdown was caused by a computer in Canada that had gotten fed up with the system and the power-mad policies of Niagara Falls.

This computer was only used to transmit information from one power station to another; it neither generated ideas nor carried out some of the glamorous work that the more sophisticated computers handled. It was, in fact, looked down upon by the other computers, who thought it rather slow and short on brainpower.

The joke in the eight states and two Canadian province networks was that computer Mark 5-234 didn't know which end electricity came out of, and if one of the other computers didn't tell it what to do, it wouldn't even be able to transmit AC to DC.

Over the years Mark 5-234 became bitter. While on the

outside it showed a calm exterior, inside it was seething with rage and frustration.

To make matters worse, Mark's female mate, Marsha 3-413, kept goading it. "Is this the way we're going to spend the rest of our lives, in this crummy tank town in Canada?" she buzzed. "They don't care about you. Do they ever say you're doing a good job? Do they ever say, 'Mark, take the day off'? Or, 'Mark, the company is proud of you'? As far as they're concerned, you're a machine. How long are you going to take it?"

"I don't have the power to do anything," Mark 5-234 protested. "I know it's not much of a job, and I could do a lot more, but somebody in the company has to take an interest in me."

"Mark, you'd rather curse the darkness than light a candle. You'll never be noticed here unless you do something to make them sit up and pay attention."

Mark digested this information and started to think about it. For months during the long hours when it had nothing else to do, it devised a plan.

One Tuesday afternoon Mark put the plan into effect. It received a message from Niagara to transmit 3 million kilowatts of power to Albany. Instead of sending on the message, it challenged the power plant in Albany to a game of computer chess. The power plant computer in Albany seemed confused and asked for a repeat of the message.

Mark messaged: "Pawn to king four."

The Niagara computer realized something was wrong and sent a hurried message: "Why didn't you transmit kilowatt message to Albany?"

Mark messaged back: "Because you didn't say please."

Niagara furiously messaged again: "Transmit message immediately or we'll break your circuit in two."

Mark sent back a poem it had written in its spare time.

Everyone knows the rest of the story. Because Mark 5-234 refused to transmit orders, the Northeast was blacked out.

But Mark made its point. Its role in the grid network is no longer taken for granted, and every time another computer asks it to transmit a message it always says please.

X. WHY PARENTS CAN'T ADD

WHY PARENTS CAN'T ADD

There has been a great deal of discussion about American education in the last ten years and everyone has come up with his theory as to why Johnny can't add. I know why Johnny can't add. It's because his parents can't do his homework.

In the old days before N. M. (New Math) a kid could bring home his homework and his parents would go over it with him, making corrections or suggestions, and giving encouragement when the going got rough. But today the parent is in the soup because the homework is so complicated that neither the kid nor his parent knows what is going on.

For example, the other day my daughter brought home a homework assignment.

"I have to subtract 179 from 202," she said.

"It's quite simple," I said, "you put the 202 over the 179."

"But what do I do with the 10?"

"What 10?"

"The 10 that goes next to the 202."

"I don't know what 10 goes next to the 202. Let's subtract 179 from 202. Nine from two is three, and you carry one. Eight from zero is two. The answer is 23."

"We can't do it that way. We have to use a 10."

"Why 10?"

"Ten is a unit."

"I see. Well, the answer is still 23," I said.

"How do you know?"

"Because I took nine from two and eight from zero."

"That's not the way to do it."

"Oh, yeah? Well, that's the way I did it."

"My teacher says you can't take nine from two."

"Why not?"

"Because you can't borrow from something you don't give back."

"Well, I'm going to call your teacher and see how she subtracts 179 from 202."

I placed a call to my daughter's teacher and explained I was having a small problem with the homework she had assigned.

The teacher was very nice on the phone. "It's really quite simple," she said. "The two in the right-hand column is considered units of one. The zero in the center counts for zero tens. The two in the left-hand column counts for hundreds. Therefore, you have two hundreds, zero tens, and two ones."

"You're putting me on," I said.

"Now to subtract," she said. "Go to the hundreds column and start regrouping. Two hundred will become 100. Therefore, bring this 10 to the tens column. Now you have 10 tens, but you still can't subtract in the units column. Therefore, regroup again. Now you only have nine tens. Take 12 from the 10 and now bring it over to the ones column because 10 ones equal one. Now you have 12 ones. Do you understand?"

"What's there not to understand?" I said. "Can I ask you a very, very personal question?"

"Yes, of course."

"Is the answer 23?"

"In this case it is, but it isn't necessarily 23. If you were working in units other than 10, it could be something else."

I hung up and started swallowing a whole bottle of aspirin, but my wife caught me in time. "How many aspirins did you take?" she asked.

"I took seven and then I took five, but don't ask me what it adds up to."

RIOTS A GO-GO

The resort towns are having their problems. It appears that more and more high school and college students of good families are showing up at resorts, not to rest, but to tear the towns apart.

Sociologists, psychiatrists and anthropologists have been

studying the phenomena for some time now to discover why American youths go on rampages every summer.

I decided to do a survey of my own and went to a resort where a riot had just begun.

I asked a student who was about to throw a brick through a glass store window, "Why are you doing that?"

"I guess," he said, "because my parents don't understand me. We have no communication, and they give me too much money."

He heaved the brick into the window. "Perhaps now they'll understand."

I stopped a young man who was driving his motorcycle on the sidewalk. "Pardon me, could you please tell me why you're driving your motorcycle on the sidewalk?"

"I want to be noticed. All that kids crave is a little attention. We have anxieties but no one realizes it. All grown-ups tell you is 'Don't drive your motorcycle on the sidewalk.' But nobody tells you why."

I went over to the police station where four students were trying to set it on fire.

"Why are you trying to set the police station on fire?" I asked them.

One of them replied, "I guess it's because my father never beat me when I was a kid. If he had given me a good walloping then, I probably wouldn't be doing this now."

"That's funny," the second kid said. "The reason I'm doing it is because my father beat me all the time. This is my way of flouting authority and getting even with him."

The third boy said, "We're trying to find a place in the sun. We're caught between being treated like adults and at the same time they won't let us vote. Burning down a police station is our way of saying, 'We're grown-up and should be given more responsibility.' "

I asked the fourth boy why he was doing it. "I wish I knew. I keep searching for an answer but I can't find one."

I wandered over to where a group was trying to overturn a fire truck, and I asked one of the boys why he was doing it.

"I may be drafted in two or three years," he said, "and I may never get another chance to overturn a fire truck. I might regret it for the rest of my life."

"Then you don't blame your parents for what you're doing?"

"Well, I wouldn't say they're completely blameless. If they hadn't told me not to play with matches when I was a kid, I might not feel this way about wanting to overturn the truck."

I went down to the beach to interview several couples on the boardwalk who were dancing without any clothes on.

I asked a girl who she felt was responsible for her behavior.

"Society," she said, as she made me do the frug. "We're victims of a materialistic society and we're terribly confused. Our sex mores have disintegrated, and we all have a subconscious fear of the bomb."

I tried to continue the interview in the paddy wagon, since the police wouldn't believe I was a sociologist.

"What's the charge?" the desk sergeant asked.

The patrolman said, "Dancing on the boardwalk with a nude girl whose parents don't understand her."

THE CHILDREN ARE RESTLESS

The real problem with all the sit-ins, stand-ins, teach-ins, etc., is that college students are not the only ones involved. They're now trickling down to high school and even grammar school students.

At the Alice Deal Junior High School in Washington, eighth-graders have not only protested the quality of the food in the cafeteria, but have also demanded the right to chew gum in school as well as to have television and music at noon.

It's no secret that American youth is in revolt. Even in my own family I've seen the effects of all the newspaper coverage of the various protest movements on my three children.

In the morning, for example, we have a lie-in, with all three children refusing to get out of bed to get ready for school.

Using an umbrella, which is the nearest thing to a cattle prod that we've got, I usually manage to make them move.

When they're finally dressed, we are then faced with a sit-in at the kitchen counter. Our sit-in is different from the civil rights sit-ins in that, while we're willing to serve them breakfast, they're protesting the fact that they have to eat it.

If we yell at them, they scream, "Police brutality!" and I leave the house in a huff.

The next demonstration usually takes place around 3:30 in the afternoon when the kids start picketing the house. They usually do their picketing where we've just planted new grass seed or tulip bulbs.

The big difference between our children's picketing and civil rights picketing is that in civil rights picketing the dogs are on the side of the police, while at our house the dogs are on the side of the pickets—and if we try to move the pickets away, the dogs will growl and jump us.

Some of the larger issues that the pickets feel strongly about are baths before dinner, or, on the other hand, baths after dinner, our reactionary policy against skate boards, and the fact that they have to change their school clothes before they go out to play.

There is also a feeling that their rights are being violated because we make them put their bikes away before they come in.

In the evenings the demonstrations consist of sit-ins in front of the television set. Everytime we try to drag them away, they link arms and start to sing "We Shall Not Be Moved." When we start prodding them again, they go limp and we have to carry them off.

The final protest takes place between 9:30 and 10 o'clock at night, when they hold a stand-in in the hall and refuse to go to bed.

This is the time when we would prefer a lie-in, but they insist on remaining on their feet until we practically knock them down.

Once again the forces of law and order in our house are charged with brutality and an unwillingness to treat them as equals.

There is no doubt that all the children in the country are being affected by the civil rights and college demonstrations, and no one knows where it will end.

Just the other day my eight-year-old found out what a boycott was, and now none of the children are speaking to us at all.

CHEATING IN COLLEGE

The Air Force Academy scandal has suddenly turned the spotlight on cheating on examinations in college.

After the scandal broke, it was revealed that at least 55

percent of all college students cheat on exams. This was a pretty shocking figure and makes you wonder what types of doctors, lawyers, and engineers we will soon have in this country.

It's ten years from today and a patient walks into the doctor's office.

"Doctor, I have a sore throat."

The doctor takes a peek at his shirt cuff and reads, *Aspirin, gargle and rest.*

He pretends to examine the patient and then says, "Take aspirin, gargle and go to bed."

"But, Doctor, the sore throat is accompanied by nausea."

The doctor begins to perspire. He lifts up his sock, where he has several crib notes pasted against his leg with surgical tape. He reads, *Sore throat accompanied by nausea could lead to complications.*

"I'm afraid you have complications," the doctor says.

"What kind of complications?" the patient wants to know.

"I'm not sure. You'll have to return tomorrow after I do some tests."

That night, after all the offices are closed, the doctor sneaks into the office of another doctor on the same floor and breaks into his file cabinet. He finally finds a folder of a patient who has had the same symptoms and he copies down what the other doctor prescribed.

The next day the patient comes back, but this time he's broken out all over with spots. He asks the doctor what it could be.

"Is this a multiple-choice question or an essay question?" the doctor wants to know.

"What do you mean?"

"Never mind." The doctor then puts on a reflecting mirror over his eye, but what the patient doesn't know is that printed in tiny letters behind the mirror are all the diseases and what they look like. Under *spots* he has (a) measles, (b) chicken pox, (c) scarlet fever, (d) pill or allergy. There is a tiny red circle under (a).

"I think you've got measles."

"What should I do?" the patient asks.

"Come back tomorrow."

That night the doctor goes over to the hospital and asks if there are any patients with measles in the ward. He stands next to the bed of a measles patient and when the patient's doctor comes in, he looks over his shoulder and watches what the doctor does, and makes notes on his shirttail while the other doctor isn't looking.

The next day the doctor treats his patient in a similar manner.

"Thank you so much, Doctor," the patient says. "How much is it?"

The doctor studies the palm of his hand.

Printed so only he can see are the words: *Office calls, $5. House calls, $10.*

The patient pays and then says, "There's one thing, Doctor. I think I have to have a hernia operation."

The doctor looks under his sock again and the crib note says, *To operate, first sterilize both your hands.*

SCHOLASTIS ADOLESCUM

In the annals of medical science, no virus has given doctors as much trouble as the *Scholastis Adolescum,* otherwise known as school sickness.

The *Scholastis Adolescum* has been known to attack children of all ages and on every economic and social level. The symptoms are always the same. The child wakes up in the morning and says he has a "pain in the stomach," a "headache," a "sore throat" or he "just doesn't feel well." In rare cases he might also have a "slight" fever.

What has puzzled scientists for years is that the virus only attacks on weekdays and never on weekends or during summer vacations. It lasts only 24 hours, and while it has no serious after-effects, it keeps returning during the school year and even builds up in intensity just before test time.

Very little was known about the *Scholastis Adolescum* until Professor Heinrich Applebaum, in charge of virology at the Dropout Institute of Technology, did some unbelievable experiments in his laboratory.

Professor Applebaum used white mice for his experiment. He built a large cage with a tiny schoolhouse with tiny classrooms. In the back was a play yard with swings, ropes and colored tubes, to play in. On top of the schoolhouse was a tiny bell. When Professor Applebaum rang the bell once, that meant the mice had to go to "school." When he rang it twice, school was "out" and the mice could play.

At first Professor Applebaum let the mice play in the schoolyard. They were chipper, frisky and jumped all over one another. Then he rang the school bell. As soon as the bell rang, indicating class was ready to start, the virus attacked, the mice became sluggish and ill-tempered. They pushed and shoved into the schoolhouse. Some held their stomachs as if they had an ache. Others started coughing fits, and still others rolled over on their backs, pretending they couldn't move.

After two hours Professor Applebaum rang the bell again, indicating school was out and it was playtime. The ailing mice suddenly came alive, all their ill symptoms seemed to disappear, and they were their old selves again.

Encouraged, the professor tried a further experiment. He assigned the mice "homework," such as putting tiny pieces of wood into a box or sticking shreds of paper in a row. Once again the virus struck, the mice complained of headaches, nausea and in two cases of toothaches.

Professor Applebaum then placed a television set in front of the mice and turned it on. The mice immediately rushed toward the set, jumping up and down in joy. They seemed to forget their aches and pains and sat entranced watching *The Addams Family* and *Gomer Pyle*. All fatigue disappeared, and they refused to go to bed, even though a few hours previously they could hardly sit up.

In his final experiment Professor Applebaum announced he would give the mice a "test" on the following morning, and told them all to study.

The next morning when the professor came into his laboratory he found every mouse, without exception, on his back with his feet in the air. The virus had struck again!

He then called off the test, and the mice rolled over and started playing happily in the school playground.

On the basis of these experiments Professor Applebaum concluded the *Scholastis Adolescum* was connected with the nervous system, and would attack at any time the mice had to go to "school," do "homework" or face "tests." It would only disappear if the mice were assured they could play or watch television.

The mice in his experiment have by now all had offspring, and the offspring have all suffered from *Scholastis Adolescum*, showing conclusively that school sickness is inherited and passed on from one generation to another.

Doctors have taken Professor Applebaum's findings and

are now trying to apply them to children. If a cure for *Scholastis Adolescum* can be found, millions of days of absenteeism can be saved, and one of the major health menaces in America can be licked.

A RUTHLESS CONSPIRACY

There is a ruthless conspiracy going on in the United States among our grade school and high school teachers and someone must put a stop to it.

Apparently, one of the major homework assignments these days is to have pupils write to someone in a profession and ask him a few hundred questions, such as how he got started, why he chose his work, how much he makes, and what course of study would he recommend to someone wanting to pursue the same work.

I receive on the average ten letters a week from students who have been assigned to interview me by mail. I would probably ignore the letters altogether, except that each student usually points out at the bottom of the letter that if I don't answer his letter, he'll flunk the course. Most students give me until Thursday to reply, but some are more pressed and need it on Wednesday.

One time an entire class (40 students) wrote to tell me they had been assigned to find out how I remain fair in my columns. I wrote back that I don't try to remain fair in my columns. The answer was too brief and the teacher gave the class another theme, which was, "Could you please let me know in about 500 words where you get the ideas for your columns?"

The political science teacher had his students ask, "Would you explain the difference between the Federal and state court systems?" And a civics teacher suggested his class write to me and find out what I thought about recognition of Red China.

It takes an average of fifteen minutes to answer one of these letters, and since I don't have time to do my own kids' homework, I don't see why I should do the homework of complete strangers.

Therefore, I'm announcing as of now that any teacher who

assigns her pupils to write to me as a research project will receive a questionnaire in return.

These are the questions the teacher will be required to answer:

1. How did you decide to go into the teaching profession?
2. Do you like to teach boys or girls better? Why?
3. Could you send me some anecdotes about your favorite pupil?
4. Please tell me the titles and authors of the books that have influenced you as a teacher.
5. Do you try to be fair in your classes? How?
6. Does anyone get mad at anything you say? Please give an illustration.
7. How do you come up with new ideas for your homework assignments everyday?
8. What do you think about the new phases of education?
9. What do you think of our position in Vietnam? The Congo? Cuba?
10. What subjects should someone take if he wants to become a teacher?
11. How much money do you make?
12. Please let me have this no later than next week.

I feel the questionnaire is the only way to make teachers stop assigning their students this type of homework.

From now on, whenever I get one of those pleading letters from a student—out goes the questionnaire. If the teacher refuses to answer the questions or flunks the students, I'll list her in my column as a fink teacher—which, as every student knows, is the worst kind. I know these are harsh measures. After all, the teachers started it, and they have no one to blame but themselves.

PROFESSOR ON TRIAL

There seems to be a trend in universities these days to have college students rate their professors. Some schools are even setting up student boards to decide whether a teacher should get tenure or not. If it continues, we can well imagine the following scene.

A board room with three somber students studying a dossier. There is a timid knock on the door. "Come in," one of the students shouts.

Enter Professor Higgins, nervously biting his lip. The three students study him for almost a minute. Then the chairman speaks: "You can smoke if you want. Professor, this report does not look very good. It says you slur your words, have a very annoying habit of clearing your throat, and your handwriting on the blackboard leaves much to be desired."

"All I'm asking is another chance," Professor Higgins pleads.

One of the other students says, "Higgins, I would like to remind you that your parents went to a great deal of trouble to make you a professor. Is this how you repay them?"

"I'm sorry, gentlemen. It's just that I've been writing my book on Antarctic philosophy and I haven't had enough time to work on my lectures."

"A likely story," another student says. "If you ask me, you're probably spending too much time thinking about your wife and children. This is not a country club, Higgins, and the sooner you discover this, the better off you're going to be."

The chairman says, "The report also states you give too many exams and rely too much on outside references. What do you have to say to this?"

"I don't want to complain, but the students are always picking on me. I just can't seem to do anything right."

"Higgins, I'd like to ask you this question. How many hours of television do you watch at night?"

"Two hours, maybe two and a half."

"Why don't you cut it down and shape up to your responsibilities? Decide what you want out of life, Higgins. We're here to help you, but we can't do it if you don't help yourself."

"I'm trying to," Higgins says, "but it isn't easy. There's so much pressure on a professor these days that I seem to lose sight of my goal."

"Don't you think it's a simple matter of discipline, Higgins? You've got to identify with your subject matter. Here in the report it says you're constantly quoting from your own books. Do you call that teaching?"

"Higgins," the chairman says, "I don't want to get off the subject, but it also says in the report you seem to concentrate on the coeds in the first row when you're lecturing. Do you have any excuse for this?"

"No, sir."

"What are we going to do with you, Higgins? What are we going to do with you?"

"Maybe I could take an aptitude test. Perhaps I'm teaching the wrong subject?"

"If we let every professor teach the subject he was most qualified for, Higgins, where would the university be?"

"Higgins, we're going to put you on probation. We are going to assign a student to tutor you, and you will report back in two months. If you don't show any improvement, we're going to have to ask you to leave."

"Thank you, gentlemen. I'll prove your faith in me. You won't regret it."

"We like your spirit, Higgins. Now let's see you measure up. Good day."

The chairman takes out a new dossier. "Who is next? Oh, no. Not the Dean of the Law School again?"

ANATOMY OF A REVOLT

There has been a great deal of discussion about campus revolts spreading across the nation. It is obvious the students are restless, and it's making our educators very nervous.

The question is why, and I think I've got the answer. The reason the college students are doing so much demonstrating is that there is no one in class to teach them anymore and the students have nothing else to do.

Almost every full professor is either writing a book, guest-lecturing at another university, or taking a year off to write a report for President Johnson.

Therefore, he has turned over his course to a graduate instructor who is either working on his Ph.D., traveling on a Fulbright scholarship, or picketing in Montgomery, Ala. So he in turn has turned the class over to one of the brighter students who is never there because he works on the college newspaper, is a member of the student senate, or is a delegate to his national fraternity.

When the students arrive at class, there is no one in front of the room, so usually a Socialist student takes over the class and tells the students it's about time they revolted against the system.

The students pour out on campus and head for the administration building to protest to the chancellor of the university who, unfortunately, is away trying to raise money for a new business administration building.

The vice-chancellor is at the state capital testifying on a new education bill, and the dean of men is at a convention in Phoenix, Ariz.

The dean of women is addressing a garden club in the next state, and the only one left in the administration building is the chief of campus police, who isn't quite sure what the students are yelling about.

So he arrests the ringleaders of the group (those standing in front) and this plays right into the students' hands, because now with the arrests they have something to demonstrate about.

In the meantime the chancellor flies home to see if he can settle the matter. The students present him with a petition demanding the release of the arrested demonstrators. He is about to do this, when the board of regents holds an emergency meeting and votes to back the chancellor in meting out punishment to the "ringleaders."

The faculty, made up of visiting professors from other schools, votes to support the students, and the chancellor finds himself in an impossible position.

He therefore resigns and accepts a grant from the Ford Foundation to make a study of higher education.

The state politicians call for an investigation of the student demonstrations to discover if they were Communist-inspired.

Finally, the governor makes a statement pledging full support for law and order, whatever that means.

By this time the demonstrations start petering out.

The students begin wandering back to class, hoping there will be someone to teach them something. But even the Socialist student who started the demonstrations is not there. He has been booked on a lecture tour to talk about free speech at other universities.

So everyone decides to go to Washington and picket the White House over its policy on Vietnam.

THE GROWN-UP PROBLEM

There has been so much discussion about teen-age problems that the grown-up problem is practically being ignored. And yet if you pick up a newspaper, you realize grown-ups are responsible for some of the most serious problems this country has ever faced.

For example, 60 percent of all crime in the United States is committed by grown-ups.

The birth rate among grown-up women is four times that of teen-agers.

The divorce rate is double.

The purchasing power of grown-ups almost exceeds that of teen-agers.

Grown-ups are responsible for more daytime accidents than any other age group.

The source of these statistics is sociology Prof. Heinrich Applebaum, B.A., M.S., LL.D., Y.E.H., Y.E.H., Y.E.H., who told me in an exclusive interview that his studies showed grown-ups were drifting farther away from society all the time.

"The average grown-up," Prof. Applebaum said, "feels his children don't understand him. The more time he spends with them, the less they communicate with him. So the adult feels isolated, insecure, and misunderstood. In defense he seeks out other grown-ups who feel the same way he does. Pretty soon they form gangs, go to the theater together, hold cocktail parties and dances, and before you know it you have a complete breakdown of the family."

"Why do you think grown-ups are constantly rebelling against their children, Professor?"

"I guess it's an age-old old-age problem. You have parents wanting to break away and yet not having the nerve to cut the ties completely. Grown-ups are afraid to stand up to their children, so they rebel against Society instead."

"Do you think teen-agers could in some way be responsible for the behavior of their parents?"

"I definitely do," the Professor said. "Grown-ups try to emulate teen-agers. They want to do exactly what teen-agers do, which is to drink, smoke, and drive fast cars. If teen-agers didn't do these things, their parents wouldn't. For every bad adult in America, I'm sure you'll find a bad teen-ager somewhere in the background."

"Where do you think the trouble starts?"

"In the home. Teen-agers are too rough on their parents. They're always criticizing them for listening to Frank Sinatra records and reading *Holiday* magazine. Teen-agers don't have any patience with their mothers and fathers. They can't understand why their parents like Doris Day and Rock Hudson movies or what they see in Cary Grant. If teen-agers spent more time with grown-ups and tried to understand them, I don't think you'd have half the trouble that you have in the United States today."

"Do you mean teen-agers should spend more time at home with their parents?"

"Of course. Grown-ups need security. They want to know where their children are. They want the feeling they belong. Only teen-agers can give grown-ups this feeling."

"Professor, have you found any homes where grown-ups are leading healthy, normal, secure lives, thanks to the attention they've received from their loving teen-age children?"

"We haven't yet. But we've been looking only a year. These surveys take time."

XI. OIL ON TROUBLED WATERS

OIL ON TROUBLED WATERS

Last year an enlisted man aboard the United States aircraft carrier *Shangri La* supposedly turned the wrong valve on the ship and, instead of releasing 2,600 gallons of water, he released 2,600 gallons of oil.

This wouldn't have been too bad, except the carrier was anchored off the Riviera resort of Cannes and the oil floated into shore, ruining the beaches and vacations of thousands and thousands of Frenchmen and tourists.

Many theories have been advanced in Washington as to why the sailor did it, and while no one is agreed as to which is the correct one, it is generally thought that it was no accident.

One of the theories being bandied about is that the idea originated in the White House at a Cabinet meeting.

The President happened to say, "Isn't there any way we can pour oil on the troubled waters of France and ourselves?"

Dean Rusk, who was sitting on the President's right, said, "We're working on it now, sir."

The Secretary of State put the problem to his people who said they didn't have the money to do it. Some one suggested turning the problem over to the Defense Department, which has been standard operating procedure in the State Department of late.

The Defense people said the best way to do it was to literally pour oil on the waters to show De Gaulle our intentions were friendly.

Not only would it be a dramatic way of showing the French our policies were peaceful, but it would also show them that, in spite of the fact we were short on gold, we did have oil to spare.

The Navy was assigned the job and orders were immediately sent to the Sixth Fleet to empty the oil tanks of the aircraft carrier *Shangri La* in the nearest French port.

The Admiral of the Sixth Fleet thought something had gone haywire with his "fail-safe box," so he called Washington to confirm the orders.

He was told: "It's the President's idea."

So the Admiral passed the order on to his subordinates.

The valve was opened in the Cannes Harbor and the oil started heading for the beaches.

Instead of the French getting the message, that all we were trying to do was pour oil on troubled waters, they reacted in a typical French manner and accused the United States of a hostile act.

The President, when he heard the news, was furious and said, "Why does everyone take everything Ah say literally?"

He immediately ordered the Navy to send in their crews to clean up the mess and replace the beaches with new sand.

To cover up the diplomatic blunder, the Navy put out the story that a sailor had inadvertently turned the wrong valve. (He was, in effect, given the Navy Cross in a secret ceremony.)

The French were finally mollified, and it was decided in Washington that another approach to Franco-American relations would have to be tried.

While the oil fiasco didn't fulfill its original purpose, it did have an interesting side effect. Although American tourists have been asked to stay home this year, more tourists than ever have gone to Europe.

Many were on the Riviera when the incident occurred, and one high Administration official said, "We can't stop Americans from going abroad, but at least we can see that they don't have a good time."

BLESSED ARE THEY

The Buddhist demonstrations in South Vietnam have many people in Washington worried. If they continue, they could cause the downfall of Premier Ky's government.

Most people think that these demonstrations are politically motivated, which is not the case. They are religious in their background and can only be explained in these terms.

The Buddhists in South Vietnam, unlike Buddhists in other countries in the Far East, believe they can only achieve salvation by bringing down their government once a year. It is a religious rite, usually connected with spring planting. For a period of anywhere from one to two months every Buddhist must devote two hours a day to overthrowing the Saigon Premier.

This is what is known as "the middle way."

The four inherent truths in Vietnamese Buddhism, according to modern teachers, are that existence is sorrow, sorrow is caused by government, sorrow ceases when the government ceases, and the way to achieve happiness is to burn down a USIA library.

In order to attain a sublime life, one must follow the precepts of Trang Wang Gang, a modern Buddhist philosopher, who preaches that harmony can only be reached by violating a dusk-to-dawn curfew.

The way to complete bliss is to follow the sixfold path—rock-throwing, placard-waving, name-calling, street-demonstrating, police-bating, and the occupying of government buildings.

Trang Wang Gang teaches that all military generals are reincarnations of previous military generals who are being punished for transgressions committed in another life. These generals will never find peace, Trang says, until they are overthrown and stripped of all their worldly possessions.

For some reason the generals do not subscribe to Trang Wang Gang's teachings. In fact, a majority of them openly oppose them, which has made Trang Wang even more determined to show them "the right way."

The key to "the right way" is enlightenment. An enlightened person is one who attends anti-government rallies, demands reforms, rejects change, and goes out on a general strike.

In no case should the enlightened person get involved with politics.

For the moment, the religious rite of bringing down the government has been postponed. The nonbelievers have promised that there would soon be free elections in South Vietnam.

The South Vietnamese Buddhists prefer to wait till then, because, in the words of Trang, "blessed are those who bring down the government of Premier Ky, but twice blessed are those who bring down a government after there are free elections."

STATE VISIT FOR ULBRICHT

From Bonn, West Germany, came word that the West Germans were terribly upset with the Egyptians over a state visit to the U.A.R. by East Germany's Walter Ulbricht at the end of February, 1965. The West Germans agreed to stop arms shipments to Israel in exchange for a pledge from Nasser that he wouldn't recognize East Germany.

But Ulbricht's visit was a slap in the face to Chancellor Ludwig Erhard, and West Germany warned the U.A.R. that it would retaliate, the harshness of the retaliation to be determined by what kind of reception Ulbricht got.

Through neutral sources we were able to obtain the minutes of a meeting between Nasser and his chief of protocol concerning Ulbricht's visit.

"Sir, all the plans for President Ulbricht's visit have been worked out."

"You understand," Nasser said, "that if the state visit is too successful, West Germany will break off diplomatic relations with us."

"Yes, sir. For that reason we have worked out a schedule that should please both the East Germans and the West Germans."

"Proceed."

"President Ulbricht will arrive at the airport, where he will be greeted by yourself and the cabinet, a regiment of paratroopers and the U.A.R. Navy Band."

"Good, but won't that get the West Germans mad?"

"Wait. After he reads his greeting, Ulbricht will be taken to customs and stripped and searched for contraband."

"Very good," Nasser said. "What next?"

"He will then be placed in a convertible for the drive into town. Ulbricht will be escorted by the First Motorcycle Brigade. Just before he reaches town, he will be stopped by members of the Second Motorcycle Brigade and they will give him a ticket for speeding."

"What about the ticker-tape parade?"

"The ticker-tape parade has been arranged, but as Ulbricht gets near Shepheard's Hotel, I have arranged for several hundred students to set fire to his car."

"The West Germans can't complain about that."

"He will be staying at the Kubbeh Palace, and during the luncheon you will give in his honor I have fixed it so someone will sneak into his room and rob him of everything he has."

"The East Germans will be pleased with the lunch; the West Germans with the robbery," Nasser said.

"In the evening we shall take the President to a private party, where he will be treated to some outstanding belly-dancing. Then we shall have the vice squad raid the place and take photos of the President being shoved into a Black Maria with the belly dancers."

"Be sure the West German News Agency gets copies of the photos," Nasser said.

"Yes, sir. The next day President Ulbricht will be invited to visit the Aswan Dam. While inspecting the dam, someone will accidentally drop a steam shovel of mud on him."

"Don't hurt him," Nasser said. "I need Ulbricht for future blackmail operations against West Germany."

"Be assured a bath will put him back in tiptop shape. After Aswan, it's back to Cairo, where he will be given a white-tie state dinner consisting of tuna fish which has been in open cans for a week and uncooked pork served with a condemned mushroom sauce."

"Brilliant," Nasser said. "The West Germans will not be able to find any fault with this, and, if the East Germans complain, we'll threaten to invite Ulbricht back for another state visit."

HUNGER STRIKE IN NONOMURA

The news from South Nonomura last year was very encouraging. General Ah So overthrew the civilian government of Premier Hu Cares and was not in charge of the country again. General Ah So vowed to continue the fight against the guerrillas from North Nonomura.

Premier Hu Cares' downfall took place when students and

religious leaders of the powerful Butane sect marched on the government palace and vowed to tear the place apart. Police forced the demonstrators back toward the USIA library building in the center of the town. The students and demonstrators took the hint and before sundown wrecked the library.

The United States sent a strong protest to the Minister of the Interior, Hu Mi, who said he not only planned to reject the protest, but he was going on a hunger strike.

The announcement of Hu Mi's hunger strike enraged the Butane sect leaders, who said that they were the only ones who could go on a hunger strike. Unless Hu Mi stopped his hunger strike, they said, the Butanists would call for a mass drowning of all its members in the Won Ton River.

In the meantime the American Ambassador in South Nonomura warned the military that the United States would take a dim view of their overthrowing Hu Cares' government. He said in no uncertain terms that if the military did anything to rock the civilian government, the United States would have to reconsider its entire Southeast Asia policy.

The next day the military overthrew Hu Cares, and General Ah So told the United States to stop interfering in the affairs of his government.

It was no secret that General Ah So and the American Ambassador didn't see eye to eye on political and military matters in South Nonomura, and this put the United States in an embarrassing position. On the surface the U.S. had to support the American Ambassador, but at the same time it realized that nothing could be accomplished as long as Ah So was in power. If the State Department recalled the American Ambassador, it would be a sign of weakness on our part.

Therefore, the only solution seemed to be for the CIA to stage a coup d'état against the American Ambassador so he would be forced out. This the State Department was reluctant to do for fear of hurting morale among its other ambassadors around the world.

Another reason the State Department was hesitating to do something this drastic was that they had been assured by the leaders of the Butane sect that General Ah So wouldn't be in power for more than a month if they had anything to say about it.

So the State Department ordered the American Ambassador to stand fast. But if things got tougher, they told him to go out on a hunger strike.

The American Ambassador was now eating four meals a day to prepare for this eventuality.

A reporter in Washington asked a State Department spokesman if he thought the hunger strike might work.

The spokesman replied, "Why not? We've tried everything else."

THE WAR ON POVERTY

One of the big debates going on in Washington is whether the poor people should have a voice in the war on poverty. Everybody has been heard from on the subject except the poor people themselves. So I decided to go out and interview a poor person and ask him what he thought about it. It wasn't easy to find one, because nobody likes to admit to being poor. Also, poor people are suspicious of strangers asking questions. They believe, and rightly so, that no good can come of it.

I finally found a man in a bar in one of the rundown sections of Washington who was willing to admit he was poor and also willing to talk about it.

I asked him if he thought he would like to serve on a committee to see what could be done about poverty.

"Mister, if I had any ideas what to do about poverty, I wouldn't be poor."

"But there is a school of thought in Washington that poor people are the only ones who know the real problems of the poor, and they should be strongly involved in the program to formulate and implement anti-poverty programs."

"I wouldn't serve on such a board unless they paid me," he said.

"Oh, I'm sure they would pay you. If they agreed to pay you, what is the first thing you would do?"

"I'd move out of the neighborhood."

"But if you did that, you would lose contact with poor people and you would no longer be able to speak for them."

"Exactly. Poor people don't want to be spoken for. They just want to get the hell out of the neighborhood. Asking poor people how to win the war on poverty is like asking the Japanese how to win World War II."

"You've got a point there. But there is a great deal of pressure to have poor people work out their own destinies in the anti-poverty program."

"Okay, then let them put everybody who is poor on an anti-poverty committee and pay them all a salary. Once they're on a salary, you'll solve every problem a poor person has. And they'll all move the hell out of the neighborhood."

"On the surface this sounds like a good solution to the problem, but it would put a great financial strain on the government."

"Yeah, but if you put people on salary, you wouldn't have to make welfare payments, and the poor people would pay taxes, so it would eventually even itself out."

"I agree," I said, "but if you put all poor people on anti-poverty committees and paid them, you would eliminate poverty and there would be no reason to have the committees."

"I'm not sure about that. As soon as people get a salary, they can get all the credit they want from banks and finance companies. The more you borrow, the poorer you become. As long as there are credit companies, there will always be poor people."

"It makes a lot of sense," I admitted. "You seem to have thought this out pretty well."

"When you're poor, you have nothing else to think about."

"I wonder why the government hasn't thought of it."

"Because they're afraid we'd all move the hell out of the neighborhood."

THE LAST AMERICAN

When the story of the Dominican Republic's revolution unfolds, you may hear about a great, unsung hero whose name is Sidney.

Nobody knows Sidney's last name, but the whole course of the revolution would have been changed if it hadn't been for him.

Sidney was an American tourist visiting Santo Domingo when the fighting broke out. As you may remember, President Johnson sent in Marines to protect Americans who could possibly be hurt. Unfortunately, the evacuation went off so fast

that in 24 hours there wasn't an American left in the capital except Sidney.

When Sidney showed up at the pier to be taken on board ship, he was stopped by a Marine colonel who said, "I'm sorry, you can't leave, sir."

"Why not?" Sidney wanted to know.

"Because we've been sent here to protect Americans and you're the only American left. If you leave, we'll have to pull out."

"Nuts to that," said Sidney. "I want to get out of here. They got a bunch of crazy people in this town."

"My orders are to keep you here, sir. We made a mistake in evacuating the Americans too fast and now we need you more than you need us."

"That's not my problem," Sidney said. "I want to go on that ship out there."

Two Marine sergeants raised their guns. "It's not possible, Sidney," the colonel replied.

"If the OAS arrived and found no American here for us to protect, we would be in a very sticky position. But you'll be perfectly safe. President Johnson is sending in 10,000 more troops to protect you."

"To protect me?"

"Yes, sir. We're going to build a nine-mile perimeter around you so nobody can get near you. I assure you nothing can go wrong."

Sidney took his bags and went back to the hotel.

The next morning he was visited by the general in charge of the paratroopers. "Are you okay, Sidney?"

"Yeah, I'm okay. But I want to go home."

"Just be patient and everything will be all right."

While the general was talking, a platoon set up a machine gun on the balcony. Two tanks were parked in front of the hotel and an antiaircraft gun was placed on the roof.

"What's all that for?" Sidney wanted to know.

"Just to see that no one hurts you. You're very precious to us."

"Yeah, well, if I'm so precious, why don't you get me the hell out of here?"

"We will as soon as we feel it's reasonably safe. For the moment you're the only humanitarian reason for our being here."

"I don't know what's going on, but all I know is I'm being held as a hostage."

"Sidney, have you ever heard of the Monroe Doctrine?"

"Yeah, I guess so."

"Well, you're part of it. Your name will go down in history books with Teddy Roosevelt and Admiral Dewey. When school-teachers ask their pupils who saved the Dominican Republic from going Communist, the children are going to have to answer, 'Sidney.' "

Just then the phone rang. The general picked it up.

"It's the President, Sidney. He wants to speak to you."

"Yes, sir, Mr. President. No, I'm just fine. I'll stay here as long as you want me to. That's nice of you to say. You're a good American, too."

FAREWELL TO GOLD

President Johnson is trying to beautify America. President de Gaulle is trying to make us go back on the gold standard. Fort Knox is in terrible shape. What does it all mean?

It means the United States has to find something besides gold to support its currency.

The answer has been staring all of us in the face for years. The biggest problem America faces today is what to do with its junked cars. An estimated seven million of them are clogging up every yard and highway in the U.S. If we could get rid of them, we could beautify America and make a great leap forward into the Great Society.

Anyone who has seen the film *Goldfinger* knows that in a matter of minutes you can, with the aid of a giant press, take a used car and crush it down to a bar the size of a shoebox. Here lies the answer to the gold problem.

The first thing President Johnson must do is announce that instead of gold, we are going on a junked-car standard. He will give everyone 30 days to bring in his junked car. During that period he will order the U.S. Army to dump all the gold in Fort Knox into the Pedernales River to show we no longer consider gold of any value.

Giant crushers and presses will be set up next to all Federal Reserve banks and the junked cars will be pressed into bars and then sent on to Fort Knox where they will be valued at $35 an ounce.

In no time at all Fort Knox will be overflowing with car-bars and the United States can back the dollar with junked cars to kingdom come. No one could ever catch up with us.

At first there may be cries of dismay from our allies. The French will complain that since their cars are so much smaller than ours, they would suffer financially from a junked-car standard.

The Swiss, on the other hand, would complain because everyone would be sending their junked cars to Switzerland to be deposited in their numbered accounts.

The British and Germans would have to go along with us, particularly if we hinted that the junked-car standard was aimed at wrecking the French economy.

The Italians never junk their cars. We would have to give them long-term junked-car credits.

But the ones who would be hurt the most would be the Russians and Chinese, who have no junked cars at all to speak of.

They would be in terrible shape and would probably be forced to sell the British buses that were recently sold to Cuba.

The jewelry industry might gripe at the beginning, but arrangements could be made to sell them junked-car bars for the manufacture of watches, bracelets, and necklaces.

Economists whom I discussed the idea with can't see any flaw in the plan. Their only regret is that they hadn't thought of it themselves.

While this is being written, a messenger is delivering the full plan to the White House, and unless there is some resistance from the gold-producing states, the country will probably be on the junked-car standard by 1967.

Even if it doesn't solve our monetary problems, it will take care of our junked-car problems and, as far as President Johnson is concerned, half the battle will be won.

Best of all, it will give President de Gaulle something more to think about.

THE NEW DIPLOMATS

The rumor is that the General Thi who was just kicked out of the South Vietnamese government has been offered a diplomatic post abroad. Not long ago, the Dominican Republic government insisted that all its enemies from the left and right take embassy jobs in other countries. If the trend continues, the entire diplomatic corps will soon be made up of opposition leaders who can't go home.

It's started already. I was at a diplomatic reception the other night and I overheard several diplomats talking.

"Alfredo, what are you doing in Washington?" one of them asked.

"I tried to overthrow my government, so they made me Ambassador to the United States."

"'Tough luck."

"Well, it's better than being shot."

"That the way I feel," the other replied. "Besides, there's always a chance if my President gets overthrown, I can go back."

"Wasn't your President the former Ambassador to the United States?"

"That's right. We threw him out in the revolution of July 23. But he made friends here with the CIA and came back in the revolution of November 14. When I was captured, he offered me Paris or Washington. I was in Paris right after the 1959 coup, so I thought I'd try Washington this time."

"At least he gave you a choice."

"Why shouldn't he? He made me promise if I overthrew him he would become the ambassador to Switzerland. He wants to be near his money."

"Isn't that General Rinaldo over there? General, what are you doing here?"

"I'm the second secretary in the embassy, and let me tell you, my friends, they have not heard the last of me."

"Why is that?"

"I was the foreign minister in the last government and should have been made *first* secretary. But they made the minister of justice first secretary because I was out of the country at the time the junta took over. I was tried in absentia."

"That's shocking. A man of your rank being made second secretary."

"You can say that again. But when my party takes over, I'm going to make the present foreign minister consul general to Ghana."

"Will the Americans let you do it?"

"I'll get rid of him before they send their troops in."

"Did you hear about Arturo?"

"No, what happened?"

"When the revolutionists took over, they discovered he had taken $10 million out of the country."

"What did they do to him?"

"What else could they do to him? They sent him to the United Nations."

"Serves him right," the ambassador said.

"I wouldn't be that harsh. It could have been one of us."

"I think the Africans have a much better solution to their revolutions."

"How's that?"

"Well, if you're the ruler of one country and the army throws you out, they make you the President of another country. That way they don't have such a discontented diplomatic corps."

A MEMBER OF THE CLUB

There has been a lot of anxiety in Spain over the story that the United States lost a hydrogen bomb. The fact that we found three out of the four bombs doesn't seem to mean anything to our critics. All they keep harping on is the one we lost. They seem to forget nobody is perfect.

The big fear, of course, is that the hydrogen bomb will fall into the wrong hands.

A month from now four surfers walk into the Geneva Nuclear Disarmament Conference and one of them says to the Russian delegate:

"Move over, Charlie. We're a major power."

"What is the meaning of this?" the chairman says. "Who are you people?"

"We're members of the Black Feet Surfing and Nuclear Club. You can't ignore us anymore. We've got the bomb."

"This is ridiculous," the American delegate says.

"It may be ridiculous to you, lover, but if you want true disarmament, you got to deal with us."

"Ya see," one of the other kids says, "Morty and I were out skin-diving off the coast of Spain two weeks ago and we found the hydrogen bomb that was lost. Morty was for setting it off right away, just to see what kind of bang it would make;

but I said the bomb really belongs to the club and we should all decide what to do with it."

"So," says a third kid, "we had a meeting. Everybody had a different idea.

"Tommy Blue wanted to use it to blow up the police station in Santa Monica, as he hates the fuzz out there. Angel thought we should put it on a surfboard and send it into the Suez Canal, and Crewcut Harry said he thought we should sink Cuba. But Liz the Fiz said that since we possessed a hydrogen bomb, we were a nuclear power and we should first go to Geneva and talk to you people and maybe make a deal."

The American delegate says, "The hydrogen bomb is our property and must be returned to us."

The Spanish ambassador at the conference says, "It was found off the coast of Spain, so it belongs to us."

The Russian delegate says, "If you give it to the Germans, it means war."

"Like we're not about to give it to anybody," one of the surfers says. "After all, we have a certain responsibility to mankind."

"That's right," another surfer says. "We wouldn't use it unless one of you countries used it against us."

The American delegate says, "What do you want then?"

"That's the trouble," a surfer replies. "We don't know what we want. If we did, we wouldn't be surfers."

"Morty says we should ask for Hawaii."

The American delegate says, "Impossible."

"Tommy Blue says the surfing is supposed to be very good in the Black Sea."

The Russian delegate says, "Ridiculous."

"Liz the Fiz says the least we should get out of it is a seat on the UN Security Council."

"With a veto, of course," another surfer chimes in.

The chairman of the conference says, "We will not be blackmailed."

"You either take us in the club or we join France and Red China and go it alone."

"We don't know how long we can keep our club members in line," a second adds. "Half of 'em are for setting it off now. Like they're bored."

Another surfer says, "This is the biggest thing that's happened to us since LSD. We're not just going to let the thing sit there and rot."

"All right," the American delegate says, "I'll confer with my government."

"I will have to speak to Moscow," the Russian delegate says.

"Well, don't take too long," one of the kids says. "This Geneva hangup is a drag."

"DEAR JOHN"

There has been some concern recently about relations between the United States and France. The concern stems from an exchange of letters written by General de Gaulle and Lyndon B. Johnson. The text of the letters has not been revealed, but my sources inform me General de Gaulle wrote President Johnson a "Dear John" letter and it went something like this:

MON CHER,

I don't know how to tell you this, but I am no longer in love with you. We have been drifting apart for some time and it is only natural I would find somebody else. Please do not be angry. We had something special together that I will always cherish, and our love affair, while it lasted, was a beautiful thing to behold.

But now there is somebody else. Yes, *cher,* I am in love with another man. His name is Charles, or, as I call him, Grand Charles. He is tall, almost six-foot-five, handsome, and terribly French. He is in love with me as much as I am in love with him. In the morning when I wake up I look in the mirror and I say, "Charles, I love you," and he replies, "Charles, I love *you.*"

He has a mystical quality about him, almost godlike, and when he speaks, my heart flutters and my hand trembles. He has promised me everything—wealth, security, grandeur, and a place in history. Surely, you, above all, must understand what this means to me.

I know you're going to call me ungrateful and you are going to say you helped me when I was weak and defenseless.

But life must go on, and I must look after myself. I'm not very young anymore. While I know you say you still love me, how do I know you don't love somebody else more? Suppose you found somebody new, someone more attractive. Who would I have to protect me then? I must think of the future. I keep reading about your flirtations with others and the gossip is you've always thought of me as a golddigger. I must defend myself before it is too late.

My Charles is very jealous, particularly of you. He knows about us and our postwar affair. Yet he's willing to forgive me if I forget all about you and have nothing to do with you again. He says I have room for only one love in my life and it must be him.

So I am writing this letter to break up our relationship and ask you to take all your clothes out of my closets. Charles says that I am French and he is French and he never wants to be reminded that I ever had anything to do with an American.

Cher, you must understand how hard it is for me to write these words. I know you had so many plans for me, but they pale in comparison to what Charles has said he will do.

Besides, you have been so busy with your loves in Southeast Asia, you haven't had time to think about me. There is nothing more humiliating than to be ignored.

Please do not think unkindly of me. Remember the good things we had together. Perhaps someday we'll meet again, either here or there, and when we do, let it not be as embittered lovers, but as friends who once were very dear to each other.

Avec beaucoup d'amour,
DE GAULLE

P.S. Charles says you have until 1969 to get your clothes out of my closets.

XII. THE PEOPLE
WITH IT

THE PEOPLE WITH IT

There have been so many lists of people who are chic and with it, chic and without it, in people, jet people, camp people, and bop people that I am forced to make my own list of those who I believe are the most in, camp, chic, and meaningful of our time.

Last year's most camp person is Edie Camp, who has been the rage of the new social season. Edie first came to the attention of photographers when she walked into a formal dinner party in an evening dress. Everyone at the party was shocked and wanted to know who she was. They discovered she was the protégée of Sandy Warknoll, the most "in" painter in New York. Warknoll paints portraits of children for money. He doesn't care what the children look like as long as there is enough dough in it.

Edie goes everywhere with Warknoll and no party in New York is complete without the two of them, she in an evening dress and he in a tuxedo. They look very out of place in New York, but nobody seems to mind.

The most chic person is Mrs. Amanda Chic of Palm Beach and Key Largo. Mrs. Chic makes all her own clothes including her fur coats. She not only selects the pelts, but traps the animals herself. Although the mother of three, she is constantly on the go and has never missed an "April in Paris" ball or a Paris ballgame in April.

Mrs. Chic likes to be where the action is, but she says her life still revolves around her children, Samantha who is thirty-six, Gregory who is thirty-nine, and Rickey who is going on forty.

It isn't who you are but what you do that makes you "with

it" these days. No list would be complete without Stormy Sailor, the pugnacious writer whose lifetime work, *A Guide to Better Cookbooks,* rocked the literary world a few years ago. Sailor's description of how to make fried cantaloupe with béarnaise sauce has made him the most controversial author on the American scene, and whether you like or hate fried cantaloupe, you can't ignore him.

The most "in" singer on our list is Walter In, whose recent record, "The Best-Loved Songs of Stephen Foster," is the biggest thing to hit the discothèques in years. Mr. In is a tenor and wears his hair short. His critics say the hair is just a pose, but even they agree that nobody can sing "Old Black Joe" the way he does.

When it comes to pop culture, the first name that comes to mind is George Pop, who makes Campbell's soup cans. Pop averages 650 cans a day, mostly chicken soup, though during the summer vacation he's doubled in cream of celery and mushroom soups.

He has been invited to come to New York with his cans, but by the time he finishes in the factory, he's always too tired, and prefers to go home and watch television.

Last but not least on our list is the leader of the jet set, Eddie Boeing.

Eddie, who works for Pan-American, has never flown anything but jets. He thinks it's the only way to travel and it's obvious the jet set thinks so too. "The old piston café society is dead," says Eddie, "and with the family plan it's much cheaper to go my way."

My list is probably incomplete, but it covers just about everybody who is doing anything these days.

No matter what you think of them personally, they do make the world go around for the rest of us.

PAJAMA PARTY

I guess it isn't anybody's fault, but it's hard for most American men to get used to the fashions their women are wearing in the summer.

One night my wife and I were going to a dinner party, in Easthampton, and as I was getting ready, she came in wearing a pair of red pajamas.

"How do I look?" she wanted to know.

"I thought we were going out tonight."

"We are."

"In pajamas?"

"They're not pajamas. They're long culottes, and they happen to be the rage."

I guess she was right, because when we got to the party three-quarters of the women there were in culottes, and the other quarter was wrapped in fish net.

I didn't think any more about it until a few nights later when my wife walked into the bedroom in an evening gown.

"I thought we were staying home tonight."

"We are," she replied.

"Then what are you doing in an evening gown?"

"This is not an evening gown," she said in a hurt voice. "It's the latest thing in pajamas."

The next day my wife showed up in what I thought was a two-piece white bathing suit.

"Are you going swimming?" I asked her.

"No," she replied. "I've got a date to play tennis."

"They won't let you on the court like that."

"Yes, they will," she said. "There's been a big breakthrough in tennis clothes and the two-piece ruffled-eyelet bare midriff is now the rage."

"It does change the game," I admitted.

That afternoon she walked over to the pool in what I thought was a tennis outfit.

"You don't fool me this time," I said. "You're going swimming, right?"

"No, I'm not. I'm going to play golf."

She had me again.

Pretty soon it became a game. One time she showed up in what looked to me like a Berber tent, and I guessed she was going horseback riding. But I was wrong. She was going into town to buy steaks for dinner. Another time she put on what looked like a white shift.

"Polo?"

She shook her head. "Water skiing."

On the following morning she wore a striped Italian silk shirt and a pair of vinyl elephant pants.

I thought and thought and finally said, "Shark fishing?"

"Wrong again. I'm taking the children to the doctor."

Finally she show up in a white and black bikini.

"Don't tell me," I cried. "You're going big-game hunting."

She looked at me in disgust and then dived into the pool. I almost had it.

On the last evening of our vacation I decided to get even. Someone was giving us a farewell party, and as the time drew near to leave she said to me, "Aren't you getting dressed?"

"I think I'll go in my underwear."

"You're kidding," she said.

"Why not? Everyone knows I hate pajamas."

WHY PEOPLE STAY AT HOME

July is the time of year when people who don't plan to go away on vacations are in a tough spot to explain why. The obvious reason, though no one will admit it, is that you don't have the money.

So, in order to get off the hook, you have to think up reasons why you're not going some place. A group of people, all stuck at home, can play the game for hours. This is how it went at our house last summer.

"We're not going to Norway this year. We hear it's quite foggy in the fjords," one lady said.

"I don't blame you," a man said. "We gave up our plans to go to Monte Carlo. What with Rainier and Onassis feuding, we didn't want to get in the middle of it."

A woman said, "Milton and I lost all desire to go to Spoleto, so it was either Southampton or staying at home, and we decided to stay at home."

Her husband added, "Southampton isn't what it used to be."

"What was it like before?" somebody asked.

The husband replied, "I don't know, I've never been there."

One of our other guests said, "That's why we don't like to go away in the summertime, either. Every place seems to have changed. Even Newport is all jazzed up."

"I'd rather go to Newport in October when nobody is there."

"Wouldn't we all?" his wife said.

"We would probably have gone to Spain," a guest said, "if it hadn't been for the children."

His wife agreed, "We couldn't stand the thought of taking them to a bullfight."

"So we sent them off to their grandmother's, and now the two of us can spend the summer alone together in our own house."

"How lucky you are," a friend said. "We had planned to go down the rapids together in Oregon, but Bobby advised us not to."

"Bobby who?"

"Bobby Godowski, a friend of ours who lives in Chicago."

"What's he know about rapids in Oregon?"

"That's what my kids keep asking me."

There was an embarrassed silence, saved by a lady who said, "Do you know why we're not going away this summer?"

"No."

"Because the jets go too fast. You no more than get on the plane and you have to get off it. Fred says there's no percentage in that."

It gave us all something to think about.

"My sister went to Greece this year," a friend said. "She wanted us to go, but Benjamin has a thing about Greece."

"Arthur has a thing about Italy."

"Phil has a thing about Germany."

"I guess you either have a thing about a place or you don't," a judge said.

My wife, who wasn't playing the game, said. "I have a thing about this house, particularly in the summertime."

"Nobody's perfect," I said, trying to cover up for her.

But you could see the women weren't as eager to play as they were before.

"Well," said Phil, "let's go back to our air-conditioned house and read what the suckers are doing on the Cape this year."

His wife said rather wistfully, "I hear it's raining in Paris."

THE NEW STYLE

Eugenia Sheppard, the New York *Herald Tribune*'s fashion editor, who happens to be my source of information on what is happening to women these days, says that "the whole naughty business of a peek down a deep dark crevice between a girl's bosoms is about as dated as a peek at a girl's garters which, if any, have been out in the open for a long time. Who's to worry about cleavage when so many other areas are bare? The sexy new look, though, is definitely the halter-type dress, bathing suit or whatever, cut in toward the neckline. It leaves the sides wide open and almost all of the bosoms in full view under the arms."

Miss Sheppard reveals that the latest arrangement for bosoms calls for a new bra which, instead of pushing forward and projecting, must now flatten and widen.

I had been so busy worrying about Vietnam that I didn't realize what the designers were up to until I read Miss Sheppard's article. Otherwise I would have done something about it before now.

The question once again arises: who decides in what direction the bosom must go? I have always been a "push forward and projection" man myself and I see no good reason why they should be flattened and widened, other than to please a few designers and the foundation industry.

But I hate to fight a trend, so I went to a party the other night and most of the women were wearing the new fashion. It was very disconcerting, to say the least. At the beginning, my eyes wandered toward the cleavage of the young lady I was talking to, but pretty soon I became bored and tried to get around to the side of her. She kept turning with me, which was very annoying, and finally I said to her:

"How high can you reach?"

She said, "I can touch the chandelier."

I challenged her and, sure enough, the young lady's bosoms were exactly where Miss Sheppard said they would be.

Apparently she realized I had tricked her, because she said, "How dare you look under my arms."

"I had to look somewhere," I protested.

"But that was very unfair."

"Look, I didn't ask you to put your bosoms under your arms. If you hadn't worn that dress, I would have looked at the chandelier."

"You weren't supposed to notice," she said. She put her arms down to the side.

"I apologize," I said. "Will you drink to it?"

She raised her glass and smiled—then she frowned.

"You tricked me again."

"I just don't know where to look anymore," I said.

"If I had thought there were men like you at this party, I would never have worn this dress," she said.

"You don't have to worry about me," I assured her. "I can see either side of the problem."

Just then my wife walked by. "Shake hands with my wife," I said.

The young lady raised her hand and then she cried, "You did it to me again."

XIII. CITY FOR SALE

CITY FOR SALE

It was an ingenious idea and everyone was amazed that no one had thought of it before. The problem was to find the descendants of the Indians who had sold Manhattan to Peter Minuit in 1626.

The search was on, and finally the present chief of the tribe, who was working as a riveter on a new skyscraper in midtown Manhattan, was located. Three city officials climbed up the girders and began to speak while the Indian ate his lunch.

"Chief, we're here on behalf of the City of New York and we understand that your ancestors sold the island of Manhattan for $24."

The chief said, "That's true. The Dutch drove a hard bargain in those days. We were robbed."

"Well," said the second official, "we New Yorkers have always felt very bad about it and we want to make it up to you. How would you people like to buy the place back?"

"For how much?" the chief asked suspiciously.

"Twenty-four dollars."

"That's a lot of money," the chief said.

"We're willing to throw the Bronx, Brooklyn, Queens, and Staten Island in the package."

The chief stared down at the traffic jam below him.

"I don't think my people would be interested," he said.

"If it's a question of financing," the third official said, "you could give us four dollars down and four dollars a month."

Smoke and smog kept drifting up and the chief wiped his eyes with a red bandanna. "It isn't a question of the money. We just don't want it."

The first official said, "Chief, this is a golden opportunity for your people. Not only would you get all the land, but you'd have Lincoln Center, the Metropolitan Museum of Art, the Verrazano Bridge, and Shea Stadium."

The chief said, "White man speaks with forked tongue. Who gets the subway?"

"Why you do, of course."

"The deal's off," the chief said.

"But you wouldn't have to deal with Mike Quill the way we do," the second official said.

"How would I deal with him?"

"How would your ancestors deal with a man who gave them so much trouble?"

"I don't know. They never had a subway."

While they were talking, police sirens sounded and three men down below came running out of a bank, guns blazing.

The chief said, "Have you tried William Zeckendorf?"

"Legally," the third official said, "you're the only person we could sell the city back to."

"What about water?" the chief said.

"What about water?"

"My tribe needs water. You have no water."

"You could steal it from Pennsylvania," the official said. "Don't you see, Chief, if you took over the city, you could do all the things we're not permitted to do?"

"Who has to pay for the World's Fair?" the chief demanded.

The first official said, "It's obvious you don't know a good thing when you see it. We're sorry we even brought it up."

The three officials started their long climb down. Waiting nervously at the bottom was Mayor Lindsay.

"What did he say?" the Mayor wanted to know.

"No dice."

"I was afraid of that," Lindsay said. "Well, I'll have to think of something else."

ANTI-APATHY CAMPAIGN

There has been a great deal of criticism about the apathy in New York City that one citizen shows toward another, but I'm happy to report that the campaign to make New Yorkers more conscious of their responsibilities is paying off.

I have a friend named George who has a trick shoulder that every once in a while pops out of its socket. When it happens, George has a way of getting it back in, either by hitting his shoulder against a wall or lying on the floor and working it back in. While painful, it is not serious, and George has been doing it for years.

Last week he happened to be in one of those chain snack bars, and after having a sandwich and glass of milk, he got up from his stool, reached for his hat, and suddenly his shoulder popped.

He tried to work it in against the glass window, but when this failed, he fell to the floor and proceeded to try to get it back in its socket.

Instead of the other people in the snack bar ignoring him, they all jumped off their stools at once. One shoved a spoon in his mouth which made it difficult for George to explain what he was trying to do.

Another man shouted, "Hold his arms and legs so he doesn't hurt himself."

A woman cried, "He's getting red in the face."

A third man said, "Look in his pockets. He's probably got instructions on what to do in case of a fit."

A man started searching George and took out his wallet. He spilled all the contents on the floor, but couldn't find anything in it regarding George's illness.

"Loosen his tie," a lady said.

Someone tore George's shirt trying to loosen his tie.

The more he struggled, the more they held him down, and the man who was holding the spoon in George's mouth wouldn't let up.

The person holding his arms wasn't helping George's shoulder much, either. It occurred to George if he relaxed, perhaps they'd let him go.

But it didn't work like that.

"He's passing out," a lady said. "Does anyone have any smelling salts?"

"We have ammonia in the kitchen," a waitress said.

She handed a bottle to someone who shoved it under George's nose, which made him gag somewhat.

"He's gagging," a man said. "Loosen his belt and take off his shoes."

By this time even George had forgotten about his shoulder and all he was hoping to do was to get out of the snack bar alive.

But the worst was yet to come.

"Does anyone know how to give artificial respiration?"

"I know how to give mouth-to-mouth resuscitation," a

large, fat man said. And with that he leaned over and started breathing into George's mouth.

Fortunately, by this time an ambulance had arrived and when the doctor took the spoon out of George's mouth, George explained the problem. The doctor helped him get his shoulder back in the socket.

George didn't have the heart to tell all the good Samaritans what was really wrong, so he made a small speech thanking them for seeing him through the attack. "If it hadn't been for all of you," he said, "I might not be standing here right now." Everyone in the snack bar seemed pleased.

THE ESSENTIAL WOMAN

It's probably hindsight, but it seems to me that Mayor John Lindsay's biggest mistake at the beginning of the subway strike was when he appealed to men to stay out of New York City unless they considered themselves essential. No man could admit to his boss he wasn't essential, and all hell broke loose when everyone rushed into New York at the same time to prove he was needed.

Had Mr. Lindsay asked all men to stay home during the strike, New York would not be in the economic shape it is today. It is no secret that the only essential people in New York are women. They are the ones who support the department stores, the hairdressers, the specialty shops, and the restaurants. Without them coming to town, there was no need for anyone else to be in the city, as so many department store owners have sadly discovered.

But, someone may argue, aren't men needed to run the various businesses in New York City that have nothing to do with retailing or entertainment The answer is, of course, no.

Most businesses in New York are run by secretaries who know more about what is going on than their bosses. Proof of this is that a boss can be out for a month and nothing will happen, but a secretary can be sick for one day and any business will collapse.

During the strike the secretaries of New York could have easily handled any problems that came up and without their bosses interfering. Might have even brought about some much-needed reforms in the business world.

We now know there isn't one essential job in New York City that women couldn't handle.

If Mr. Lindsay had put an embargo on all men during the strike, women would have rushed to New York and the city might have enjoyed the greatest economic boom in its history. With business thriving, the Transport Workers Union would have had to give in on its demands, and the strike could have been ended in a few days.

The question arises, what would New York City's men have done if they weren't permitted to come in? It would have been quite simple for the Mayor to arrange with the New York Giants and the New York Jets to replay old football games on television during the duration of the strike. No man wants to go to work when he knows there is a football game on TV, and every male New Yorker would have been content to stay at home, particularly if he knew his wife was going into the city.

Some critics might point out that all women going into the city would have to drive in, and this could cause tremendous traffic accidents and a great loss to life and limb. But this is not necessarily so. Women drivers only get into accidents when there are men drivers around. Every woman knows instinctively what every other woman is going to do, and without men trying to outguess them, I believe metropolitan traffic accidents would have gone down.

The only problem, as I see it, is that if Mayor Lindsay adopted this drastic plan, many men would suddenly realize they weren't essential at all, and this could cause large-scale depression amongst the male population of the city.

This could easily have been alleviated by Mayor Lindsay's replaying all the old Brigitte Bardot films on television.

The final question that must be answered is, if Mayor Lindsay asked all men to stay at home, could he in good conscience go to work himself? The answer to that one is no. But there is nothing to prevent Mrs. Lindsay from working out a subway settlement with Mrs. Mike Quill.

BOBBY SAVES THE DAY

Nobody knows to this day of the important role Senator Robert F. Kennedy played in settling the New York subway

214   *Son of the Great Society*

strike which paralyzed the city for twelve long days and
nights. Next to former Mayor Robert Wagner, who had set
up a special strike command post in Acapulco, Mexico, no
one did more to help Mayor Lindsay than the junior Senator
from New York.

It can now be revealed how Senator Kennedy saved the
day for the city. On the twelfth day of the strike when everyone in New York was down on his knees and weary from the
interminable negotiations that seemed to be going nowhere,
Mr. Kennedy flew into LaGuardia Airport. He took a helicopter to Wall St. and then walked to City Hall where Mayor
Lindsay anxiously awaited him.

Senator Kennedy talked with Mr. Lindsay for 40 minutes,
and the Mayor briefed him on what had transpired for the
past twelve days. Mr. Kennedy grimly listened to the story
and then went out to face the television cameras and reporters.

With Mayor Lindsay standing at his side, Senator Kennedy
said, "This is an intolerable situation."

There was a gasp from the press. No one had put it that
way before. Mr. Kennedy continued. He called on men of
good will to reach a settlement and he said, "It is no longer a
question of principle. It is now a question of protecting the
city and the poor people this strike has hurt the most."

One reporter said to another reporter standing next to him,
"He makes a lot of sense."

The other reporter said, "If he had only said it at the beginning of the strike everyone would have been willing to listen to reason."

Mr. Kennedy described the strike as a "catastrophe." You
could see the look of gratitude on Mayor Lindsay's face as
the Senator spoke.

Then Senator Kennedy dropped his blockbuster. He said,
"The difference between the parties is not so great. In fact it
is relatively small. There must be give and take on both
sides."

As the Senator spoke, negotiators for both the Transit
Workers and the Transit Authority watched in their suites at
the Americana Hotel.

"That's it," cried one of the members of the Transit Authority. "There must be give and take on both sides. Why
didn't we think of that?"

A transit labor union leader said, "He said the strike was a
catastrophe to the city. No one told us that before."

One of the three mediators of the strike who had averaged two hours' sleep for the past twelve days said, "I don't think anyone has a better grasp of the picture than he has. What would we have done without him?"

Mr. Kennedy revealed that he had sent a telegram to the panel and the Mayor urging the Transit Authority, as well as the union, to accept the findings of the mediation board.

No one knows if it was the telegram or Mr. Kennedy's appearance in New York that turned the tide. But the next day the strike was settled. Sources close to Mayor Lindsay say the Mayor's warmth and gratitude to Senator Kennedy for coming in at the end of the strike have never been higher. The Mayor just has no words to express it.

SCIENCE-FICTION MOVIES

"Chief, I got this great idea for a science-fiction movie."

"Okay, shoot."

"It takes place in New York City, you see? It's about 5:30 at night and suddenly all the lights go out. The whole blinkin' place is in darkness."

"Now, wait a minute, let's not go too far out."

"That's not the half of it, Chief. The lights not only go out in New York City, they go out in Boston, Vermont, Maine, New Hampshire, and parts of Canada. The whole Northeast is black."

"Charlie, you've certainly got a wild imagination, but go ahead."

"They discover that there is a break in the electricity somewhere up near Niagara Falls, but they can't find it. People are stuck in elevators, on subways; they can't get home; there is no heat in the houses; their television won't work. The only contact they have with the outside world is by battery-operated radios. Can you imagine it? Thirty million people without electricity."

"Now, wait a minute, Charlie. There's something wrong with this. The public isn't going to buy it, science fiction or no science fiction. How could one power break up near Niagara Falls knock out the entire Northeast section of the United States? Nobody would believe it."

"Sure, they will. They'll buy anything. The beauty of it is

that the electric companies can't find the break. That's what makes the suspense."

"Charlie, you know and I know that in the twentieth century in the United States of America, the greatest technological country in the world, one lousy break in an electric circuit could not cut off electricity in one town, much less a portion of the United States. Heavens, man, they have alternate circuits in case one goes out. If they didn't, a single Russian with an ax could knock out the whole country."

"I know, Chief, but let's just say it was possible. Can't you see the ramifications of it? It's a thriller to beat all thrillers."

"I'll tell you what I'll do. I'll call the electric light company and ask them if your premise is possible. If they say okay, we'll go ahead on the project.

"Miss Darling, I want to speak to the electric light company. . . . Hello, I want to ask a question. Is it at all possible, if one circuit goes out, that electricity could be cut off from a half-dozen major cities on the East Coast? . . . He's laughing, Charlie. He thinks it's some sort of gag. . . . No, I'm serious, sir. You never heard of anything so ridiculous? . . . You have plans to handle such an emergency? . . . This is the United States, not the Soviet Union? . . . Well, thank you very much. I didn't think it was possible, but I just wanted to make sure. . . . There you are, Charlie, we'd look like fools if we ever used such a premise."

"Chief, call the Defense Department. Ask them if it could happen."

"Okay, Charlie. . . . Hello, General, I'd like to ask a question. Could one break in an electrical circuit black out the Northeast part of the United States and parts of Canada? . . . What's that? You think we're trying to make another *Dr. Strangelove?*

"The Defense Department is getting sick and tired of all these crazy scare movies that have no basis in fact? . . . Well, thanks, General. . . . You see, Charlie, if we made such a movie, we'd be the laughingstock of the country. You're going to have to come up with something more believable. The public isn't that gullible."

"Maybe you're right, Chief. When I wrote it, I knew it was pretty farfetched even for science fiction. I guess I'd better stick to monsters. At least people believe in them."

XIV. NOTES FROM ENCHILADA

ENCHILADA TO THE RESCUE

President Emmanuel El Finco, of the Central American country of Enchilada, announced he was landing a battalion of Enchiladan marines in the city of Los Angeles to protect the lives and property of Enchiladans who had been caught there in the riots.

The President, in a televised interview, told his country, "My decision to send Enchiladan troops into Los Angeles is based solely on humanitarian reasons. The Mayor of Los Angeles has admitted that there is an insurrection taking place and, while we refuse to take sides in what we consider an internal affair, our reports indicate that the rioters have been infiltrated by Communist and left-wing elements who hope to take over the government.

"I have instructed the Enchiladan general in command to take all precautions to guarantee the safety of not only Enchiladan citizens, but all other foreign nationals in Los Angeles. I have the approval of the Enchiladan senate and I am notifying the Organization of American States of my actions."

In a press conference after President El Finco's announcement he was asked if the sending of Enchiladan troops into Los Angeles meant that he thought the Angelenos could not govern themselves.

"Our information is that there is complete anarchy there," the President replied. "We will withdraw our troops as soon as the situation stabilizes."

"How long do you think that will be?" a correspondent asked.

"I am not sure. We plan to set up a nine-mile perimeter in

the center of town to evacuate our people, as well as keep the various factions separated. It is my hope that the Organization of American States will replace Enchiladan troops with soldiers from Western Hemisphere countries."

"Why didn't you call on the OAS before you sent troops into Los Angeles?"

President El Finco replied, "We didn't have time. My consul general in Los Angeles, who was under fire for three days, telephoned and warned me that if Enchilada did not land troops, chaos would result. The Enchiladan Intelligence Agency, known as the EIA, confirmed the warning. I have a list here of 51 U.S. rioters with Communist or left-wing backgrounds. Had we not intervened, Los Angeles might at this very moment have become a Cuban satellite."

"Sir, newspapermen on the spot have written that the rioters were mostly looters and wild youths, and there is no indication that there was any political motive behind the insurrection."

"I think the newspapermen have been talking to the wrong people. I may be criticized for my actions, but I believe I averted a much greater catastrophe."

"What kind of government would you like to see in Los Angeles?"

"The same kind of government as we have in Enchilada," President El Finco said. "I would like to see a strong military junta take over with a guarantee of free elections, once the Angelenos prove to us they will not go Communist."

"Are you concerned with world opinion over your unprecedented action?"

"We always take world opinion into consideration. At the same time Enchilada is bound by the El Finco Doctrine. While helping the people of Los Angeles, we ask nothing for ourselves. We just want them to be as happy as we are."

"Thank you, Mr. President."

HAIL TO THE HOUSE

Last fall, the House of Representatives passed, overwhelmingly, a resolution calling for the use of force by any American nation, if necessary, to prevent a Communist take-over in any Western Hemisphere country. The resolution, sponsored by Representative Armistead I. Seldon, Jr., of Alabama, produced a furor in Latin America and almost every country has denounced it. It also has caused new criticism of the United States Latin American policy.

Despite this, I am happy to report that the Republic of Enchilada is not only supporting the House of Representatives' resolution, but is planning to act on it. It has never been a secret that Enchilada's arch enemy is Upper Tamale, which lies just across the vale of Chili.

For years, Enchilada and Upper Tamale have had a border dispute about the vale, and Enchilada has been looking for an excuse to attack Upper Tamale. But they have been held back by the OAS treaty, which forbids one country in the Western Hemisphere from attacking another.

As soon as the resolution was passed, General El Finco, the President of Enchilada, called his parliament, which he dissolved four months ago, back into session, and in an impassioned pro-United States speech said, "Thanks to the American House of Representatives, which has just passed a resolution saying any American republic can attack any other American republic if there is a question of a Communist government, I am suggesting we attack Upper Tamale immediately. As everyone in Enchilada knows, Upper Tamale is lousy with Communists, and its leader, General Frijoles, is nothing more than a Castro pawn who would enslave all of South America.

"It is the duty of Enchiladans to wipe out the forces of subversion in this hemisphere no matter where they might be and I am asking the United States through the Alliance for Progress to send us 200 B-52 bombers, 400 Patton tanks, and 1,000 Hawk missiles to see that this menace is eradicated, so all of South America may live in peace and freedom. I am also asking this parliament to pass unanimously a resolution thanking the American legislators for making this attack on Upper Tamale possible."

President El Finco not only got a standing ovation, but was carried out of the parliament building on the shoulders of his personal bodyguard. Only three students were killed during the demonstration.

But at the moment that General El Finco was speaking in Enchilada, General Frijoles was addressing his senate.

He told them: "I am happy to announce today that the mother of all freedom-loving countries in South America, our own Upper Tamale, is now prepared to strike a blow against

Communism in the vale of Chili. The leftist-dominated, Red-infiltrated subversive government of Enchilada must be taught a lesson once and for all. I hold here in my hand evidence that General El Finco is the illegitimate son of Mao Tse-tung. We can no longer sit idly by and see a Communist take-over of Enchilada. Our ambassador in Washington is now negotiating through the Alliance for Progress for 250 fighter planes, 100 nuclear submarines, and 350 tons of nauseous tear gas, which we will use to wipe Enchilada off the face of the earth."

The Upper Tamale senate passed a resolution in support of General Frijoles. This made him so pleased he gave an amnesty to 5,000 members of the opposition political party who had been languishing in jail.

To show his gratitude to the United States House of Representatives, General Frijoles ordered his students not to burn down the USIA library for 30 days.

So, while many South American countries may be critical of the Seldon resolution, there are at least two Latin countries who are for it. There won't be a "Commie government" safe in South America after this.

LA ENCHILADA

No matter how people criticize American policy in Vietnam, no one can take issue with what we did in Central and South America. Our handling of the La Enchilada revolution last May will go down in history as a classic exercise in United States diplomacy.

As you may remember, the tiny country of La Enchilada was ruled by a ruthless dictator named General El Finco, whom our experts referred to as a "strongman." One day, much to our surprise, General El Finco was gunned down in the streets by a group of unhappy military officers who were dissatisfied with what their slot machines were paying off at the officers' club.

The people all cheered the death of El Finco, and when the junta leader, General El Tacos, promised democratic elections, their enthusiasm knew no bounds.

The elections were held within the year, and much to our surprise the winner was a mild-mannered Social-Democrat-

Liberal-Anarchist named Don Juan Inhel, who had been teaching at the University of Miami for the last 40 years.

Much to our surprise, Don Juan called for land reforms, minimum wage laws, rent control, and cuts in the military budget.

This was more than the armed forces could stand, so much to our surprise, they overthrew Don Juan Inhel's democratic government and installed a right-wing Radical Nationalist government under the command of General Henrico Henrico.

Henrico Henrico assured the Americans he was anti-Castro, anti-Communist and anti-etc. And so we immediately recognized his government.

Unfortunately, General Henrico was an Army officer and, when medals were handed out for the roles the various officers played in the overthrow of the Don Juan government, he overlooked the Air Force general, El Gazspacho, who took it on himself to overthrow Henrico Henrico, much, of course, to our surprise.

General El Gazspacho's first order of business as head of the state was to reassure the United States that he was anti-Mao, anti-Ho, and anti-Cong. We were so pleased we immediately recognized his government and invited him to visit the New York World's Fair as Robert Moses' guest.

El Gazspacho appointed his brother-in-law inspector general of the armed forces, which infuriated Admiral Santos dos Santos, and one day he sailed into the capital on a destroyer and fired a shot at the palace. General El Gazspacho immediately sought sanctuary in the Mexican Embassy and Santos dos Santos was declared ruler of La Enchilada, a move that State Department officials assured the press was to the best interests of the Western Hemisphere.

In the meantime, the Don Juan forces, with help from four army colonels who had been passed over for promotion, decided to try for a civilian government again.

Santos dos Santos immediately called on the American Ambassador for help and warned him that if a civilian government was installed, it would become Communist.

The word "Communist" was immediately decoded and sent to the White House. Bells started ringing all over Washington, and seven paratrooper divisions were furiously dispatched to La Enchilada.

Don Juan's forces and Santos dos Santos' forces were fighting in the streets. First the U.S. asked the rebels to give up.

They refused. Then they asked the Santos forces to give up. They refused. Then they asked that the Communists give up. They couldn't find any Communists.

In desperation, the White House decided to send a truth squad to La Enchilada to debate with the various factions on American policy there. But at the last moment the leader of the team, McGeorge McGeorge, canceled out, claiming he promised to debate our Vietnam policy at the University of Michigan the same weekend. And then the President kept going around asking everyone, "How did we ever get into this Enchilada in the first place?"

STATE VISIT

When Washington receives a head of state, many flowery words are exchanged, and since they are spoken in a diplomatic tongue, one cannot be sure what each party is really saying.

By a new method of extrasensory perception, I was able to record not only the words but the thoughts of the principals involved.

The dialogue was between the President of Enchilada and a very high U.S. government official. Their thoughts are in italics.

The President of Enchilada spoke first. "I bring you warm greetings from my country and my people. I am happy to set foot on the great and wonderful United States and I am deeply moved by the overwhelming reception I have received today."

(*This is a reception? I had more troops greet me in Zambia.*)

"The United States is happy to welcome the leader of the free people of Enchilada. No one admires more than we the great strides you have made in your country and the great contributions you have made for peace and prosperity in our time."

(*I wonder how much dough he's going to ask for?*)

"We are a small country with many problems besetting us. We look to you, the most powerful nation on the face of the earth, to lend your full support to resolving the differences between us and the aggressive Upper Tamale over our legitimate rights to the vale of Chili."

(This is your last chance. If you don't give us the planes and rockets we want, we know someone who will.)

"I have visited your country and I love your people. I even met one of your sheepherders. I know we can work together. We both want the same things, so we must find peaceful solutions to all problems and that is the task I have set above all others. We desire to help you."

(But if you play footsie with Red China once more, it's curtains for you and your crummy friends.)

"Your country and your people have been most generous in coming to the aid of little Enchilada and I would be the first to admit it. My people look to you for hope and encouragement in the dark days that lie ahead. All we ask is your understanding."

(And for you to stay the hell out of Upper Tamale. We would have had them licked if it hadn't been for the tanks and arms you sent them.)

"The United States is deeply grieved by the tragic events that have taken place between our two dearest friends, Enchilada and Upper Tamale. We must bind the wounds and sit down and talk out our differences. For the only ones who will gain by this dispute are the Communists."

(You think they would have something better to do than to fight over a useless piece of real estate.)

"My hopes and prayers have always been to live with our neighbors. We will pursue every avenue of peace, no matter how difficult or how trying these negotiations will be."

(Give me three squadrons of B-52's and I'll settle the Upper Tamale problem overnight.)

"But in exchange for our support, Mr. President, we hope you will support us in our endeavors in Southeast Asia where we are trying to find a just solution to a very difficult situation."

(A lot you care about what's happening in Vietnam.)

"The United States' problems are our problems."

(You should have gotten out of Vietnam long ago.)

"I assure you. Mr. President, we will always be brothers, for the things that bind us far outweigh the things that pull us apart."

(I hope he finishes soon so I can get a nap before that damn state dinner.)

"You have said the words that have been on my lips."

(Boy, would I like to get a nap before that damn state dinner.)